creating keynote
presentations
with iwork

Visual QuickProject Guide

by Tom Negrino

Peachpit
Press

Visual QuickProject Guide
Creating Keynote Presentations with iWork
Tom Negrino

Peachpit Press
1249 Eighth Street
Berkeley, CA 94710
510/524-2178
800/283-9444
510/524-2221 (fax)

Find us on the World Wide Web at: www.peachpit.com
To report errors, please send a note to errata@peachpit.com
Peachpit Press is a division of Pearson Education

Editor: Nancy Davis
Production: Gloria Marquez
Compositor: Owen Wolfson
Cover design: The Visual Group with Aren Howell
Cover production: Owen Wolfson
Cover photo credit: iStockphoto
Interior design: Elizabeth Castro
Indexer: Rebecca Plunkett

Notice of Rights

Notice of Liability

Trademarks

ISBN 0-321-35754-X

9 8 7 6 5 4 3 2 1

Printed and bound in the United States of America

For Dori, Sean,
and Pixel the Hypnotic Cat

Special Thanks to...

My superb editor, Nancy Davis.

The book's production editor, Gloria Marquez, and the compositor, Owen Wolfson. Thanks for making this particular silk purse.

Thanks to Brian Peat for his exacting technical edit. Any errors that remain are my own.

A special thanks to the vibrant community of Keynote theme creators whose work is shown in this book: Saulius Dailide of Jumsoft (www.jumsoft.com); Jim Bradley of KeynotePro.com (www.keynotepro.com); Brian Peat of KeynoteUser.com (www.keynoteuser.com), and John Driedger of Keynote Theme Park (www.keynotethemepark.com).

My thanks to Linda Sharps of The Omni Group (www.omnigroup.com), Michael Samarin of KeyWebX (www.keywebx.com), and Brad Crystal of Nova Development (www.novadevelopment.com) for software help.

The "Choosing a College" project in this book uses the Education Pro theme from Jumsoft.

contents

contents

9. deliver your presentation 107

10. present everywhere 121

appendix: theme showcase 133

index 139

introduction

The Visual QuickProject Guide that you hold in your hands offers a unique way to learn about new technologies. Instead of drowning you in theoretical possibilities and lengthy explanations, this Visual QuickProject Guide uses big, color illustrations coupled with clear, concise step-by-step instructions to show you how to complete one specific project in a matter of hours.

Our project in this book is to create a compelling and colorful presentation using Keynote 2, part of the iWork '05 package from Apple. We will create an informational presentation designed for high school students and parents who are beginning the process of choosing a college for their sons or daughters. But because the presentation showcases all the basic techniques, you'll be able to use what you learn to create your own presentations, whether it be a talk for your annual sales meeting, a lecture for a class you're teaching, or a slideshow for your department detailing your latest work.

what you'll create

Set an interesting, colorful background theme for the slideshow.

Write your presentation in Keynote's Outline View.

Add photographs from your iPhoto library with the Media palette.

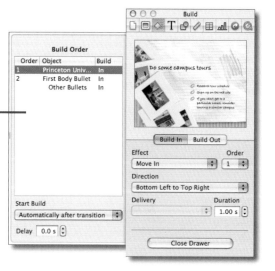

Add speaker Notes to help keep your presentation on track when you give it.

Apply slide transitions and slide builds to give your presentation movement and add visual interest.

introduction

Apply master slide layouts for each kind of slide.

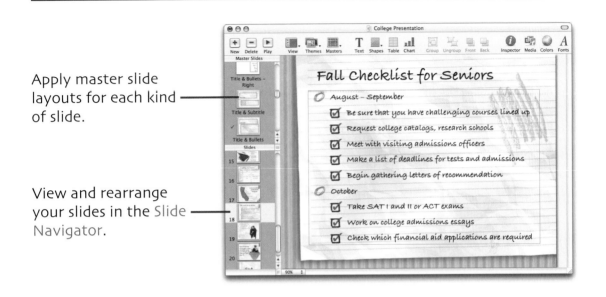

View and rearrange your slides in the Slide Navigator.

Change the look and style of text and bullets on your slides with the Inspector and Fonts palettes.

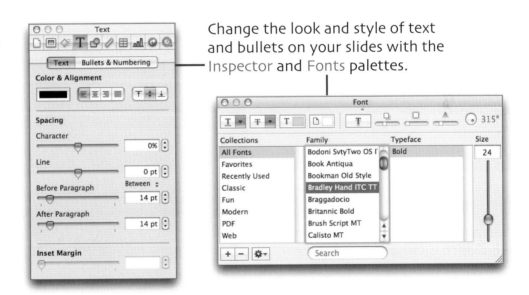

how this book works

The title of each section explains what is covered on that page.

add object builds

The generic name for an animation that occurs on a single slide is an object build. When you create a build, you can set the way the object "builds in" (appears on the slide) and "builds out" (leaves the slide). You control the build process with the Build Inspector. On that Inspector, the Build In and Build Out tabs set the build options.

Important terms and Web site addresses are shown in orange.

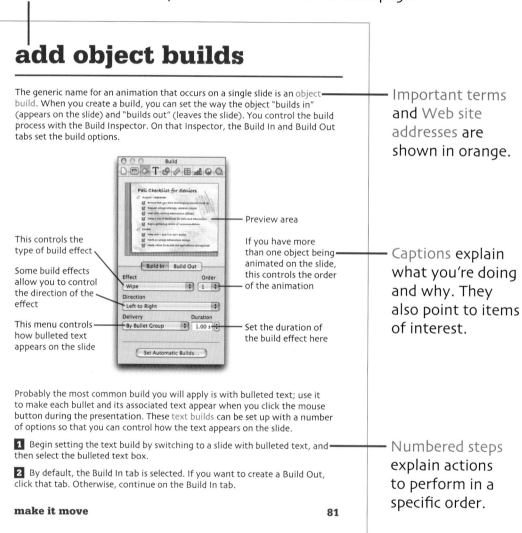

This controls the type of build effect

Some build effects allow you to control the direction of the effect

This menu controls how bulleted text appears on the slide

Preview area

If you have more than one object being animated on the slide, this controls the order of the animation

Set the duration of the build effect here

Captions explain what you're doing and why. They also point to items of interest.

Probably the most common build you will apply is with bulleted text; use it to make each bullet and its associated text appear when you click the mouse button during the presentation. These text builds can be set up with a number of options so that you can control how the text appears on the slide.

1 Begin setting the text build by switching to a slide with bulleted text, and then select the bulleted text box.

2 By default, the Build In tab is selected. If you want to create a Build Out, click that tab. Otherwise, continue on the Build In tab.

Numbered steps explain actions to perform in a specific order.

make it move 81

The extra bits section at the end of each chapter contains additional tips and tricks that you might like to know—but that aren't absolutely necessary for creating the presentation.

The heading for each group of tips matches the section title.

The page number next to the heading makes it easy to refer back to the main content.

extra bits

write the outline p. 14

- If the text in the outline is too small to work with comfortably, you can change it by choosing Keynote > Preferences, then clicking the General button in the toolbar of the Preferences window. At the bottom of the window, pick the font and font size you want from the Outline View Font pop-up menu.

use OmniOutliner p. 18

- If you're dealing with a large presentation, you have a large outline. And OmniOutliner, being a full-fledged outline processor, has better tools for working with larger outlines. For example, you have more control over the number of heading levels that you show or hide at any given time, which lets you concentrate on the points that are important without being distracted by supporting information.
- If you often use a particular design theme in Keynote, you can choose it in OmniOutliner's Preferences so that you don't have to change themes or reformat once you open the exported OmniOutliner presentation in Keynote.

work with outline text p. 16

- You can move bullets from one slide to another by dragging them out of the current slide to a different slide.
- If you drag a bullet to the left of the other bullets on a slide until a blue triangle appears above the slide, you will create a new slide containing that bullet.
- You can click and drag on a slide icon to move the slide and its contents up or down in your presentation.
- If you double-click a slide icon in Outline View, it will hide its bulleted text, showing only the slide's title. This is often useful when you are rearranging slides.
- You can also print the outline: choose File > Print, choose Keynote from the resulting Print dialog's Copies and Pages pop-up menu, choose Outline, and click Print.

write your presentation 19

the next step

While this Visual QuickProject Guide will walk you through all of the steps required to create a presentation and deliver it to an audience, there's more
to learn about Keynote. After you complete your QuickProject, consider pick-ing up one of two books, also published by Peachpit Press, as an in-depth, handy reference.

To learn more about Keynote 2, take a look at my Keynote 2 for Mac OS X: Visual QuickStart Guide.

If you want to know more about Pages, the companion program in iWork '05, check out Creating Pages with iWork: Visual QuickProject Guide, by David Morris.

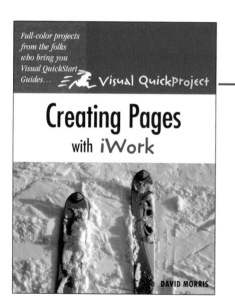

Either book will give you clear examples, concise, step-by-step instructions, and many helpful tips that will help you improve your presentations.

Another place you can go for help is the companion Web site that I've set up for this book. You'll find links to Keynote community and discussion sites, pointers to where you can find free and commercial themes for your pre-sentations, and links to some of the software that I recommend in this book. This compan-ion site (www.negrino.com/keynote-vqj/) will also be updated as needed to reflect changes in the world of Keynote.

1. explore keynote 2

Before you get started on your presentation, you need to see the tools that Keynote 2 gives you. In this chapter, you'll explore the Keynote user interface, including the main window, Inspector, Color palette, and Fonts palette. We'll go into details about buttons, menus, etc., as we need them in the project.

Start up Keynote 2. Open the Applications folder, then open the iWork folder, and double-click on the Keynote icon.

When Keynote starts, it creates a new presentation document and asks you to choose a theme from a dialog that slides down from the top of the window. For now, click the White theme, then click the Choose button. The dialog disappears and the first blank slide appears, ready for you to add content.

In this chapter, you'll create your presentation file, set it up for subsequent chapters, and save the file. You'll add text and graphics to this new document as you build the presentation throughout the rest of the book.

keynote main window

Keynote has a main document window, where you have the slide, the slide navigator (which lets you jump to the different slides in your presentation), and a toolbar.

From the toolbar, click the View button, and from the resulting pop-up menu, choose Show Rulers, and then choose Show Notes.

The Toolbar has buttons and pop-up menus with the most-used commands, such as New Slide, Play Presentation, and buttons to open the four tool palettes.

The Slide Navigator shows thumbnails of your slides, and lets you switch between your slides as you're creating them.

The Notes Field is where you can type speaker notes for each slide. These notes will appear on printed handouts and on your screen during the presentation, but the audience won't see them.

The slide is surrounded by the horizontal and vertical Rulers, which help you position graphics and text on the slide.

The Slide Canvas shows you what the current slide looks like.

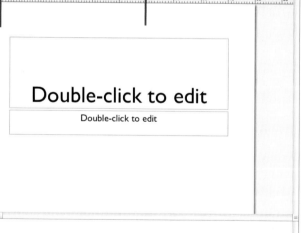

explore the toolbar

In Keynote, you'll use the toolbar to change the look of your slides and the things that you put on the slides. Here is a quick rundown of the buttons in the toolbar:

Use the New button to create a new presentation.

The Delete button removes the current slide or multiple slides you have selected in the Slide Navigator.

The Play button plays the presentation.

The Themes pop-up menu lets you select and apply a design theme to your presentation.

You use the Masters pop-up menu to view the master slides that are part of the design theme, and to apply one of them to the current slide.

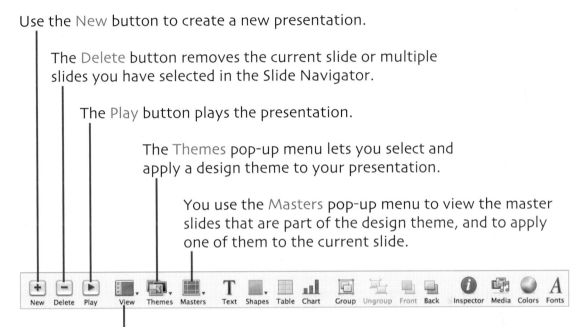

Use the View pop-up menu to switch between Keynote's three views: the Slide Navigator; the Outline, where you see a text representation of your slide content; and Slide Only view. You can also use this pop-up menu to show or hide the rulers, the speaker notes area, and the Master Slides.

explore the toolbar (cont.)

The Text button adds a new text box to the slide.

The Shapes pop-up menu allows you to add drawing objects to the slide.

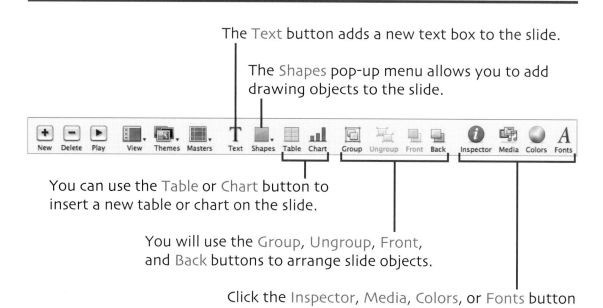

You can use the Table or Chart button to insert a new table or chart on the slide.

You will use the Group, Ungroup, Front, and Back buttons to arrange slide objects.

Click the Inspector, Media, Colors, or Fonts button to open or close their respective tool palettes.

explore the inspector

The Inspector is actually ten windows in one, and it contains most of the commands and buttons you need to modify the look of your slides and the text and graphics on the slides. It has ten different sections that affect different aspects of your presentations. You'll learn more about each of these sections as we work on the project. Here, we're looking at the Slide section, where you can control slide transitions.

The Inspector has a toolbar that allows you to select its different sections.

Slide Inspector allows you to apply animated transitions between slides; change the master slide associated with the current slide; and apply slide backgrounds.

Inspector toolbar

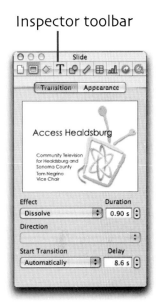

Build Inspector controls animated content on individual slides. For example, you use this Inspector to make bullet points or graphics appear on your slide.

Text Inspector gives you control over the color, alignment, and spacing of slide text, and lets you control bulleted and numbered lists.

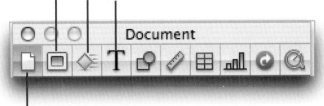

Document Inspector allows you to adjust settings that affect the whole presentation; change the slide size; and set a soundtrack for the presentation.

explore the inspector

Graphic Inspector allows you to adjust
the look of graphic elements on a slide.

Metrics Inspector allows you to adjust the
size, position, and angle of slide elements.

Table Inspector allows you to adjust
table rows, columns, and borders.

QuickTime Inspector gives you
control over QuickTime and
Flash movies.

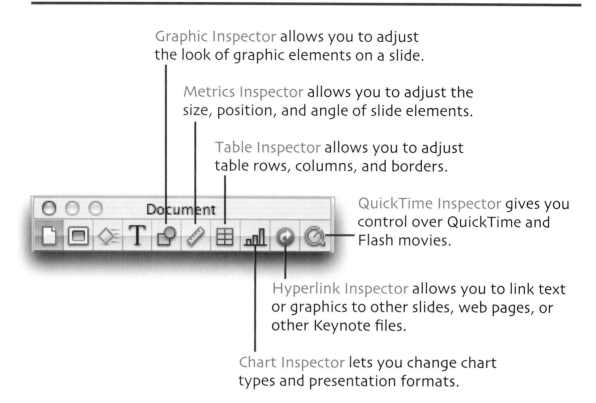

Hyperlink Inspector allows you to link text
or graphics to other slides, web pages, or
other Keynote files.

Chart Inspector lets you change chart
types and presentation formats.

explore palettes

The Media palette is new to Keynote 2, and allows you to browse images in your iPhoto library, music from your iTunes collection, or QuickTime movies in your Movies folder. Once you find the media you want, just drag it onto a slide. You'll learn more about how to use the Media palette in Chapter 6.

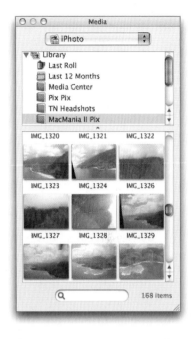

Colors toolbar

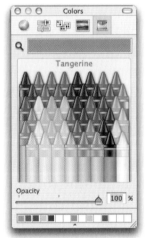

The Colors palette gives you several ways to choose colors and apply them to text and graphics on your slides. The toolbar at the top of the window lets you change between the different color methods. Here you see two of the most commonly used palettes: the Color Wheel and Crayons.

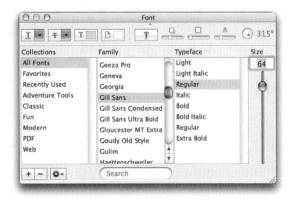

The Fonts palette allows you to choose the font family, typeface, and size for any selected text. You'll learn more about how to use the Fonts palette in Chapter 5.

keynote views

Use the Zoom menu in the corner of the slide canvas to make the slide larger or smaller.

Use the "Fit in Window" choice in this menu to make the slide fill the pane regardless of how large or small you make the Keynote window.

Keynote has three views of your presentation. You choose between the views by using the View pop-up menu on the toolbar, or by using the View menu on the menu bar.

The Slide Navigator shows thumbnails of your slides and lets you switch between your slides as you're creating them. You can also use the Slide Navigator as a visual outline of your presentation.

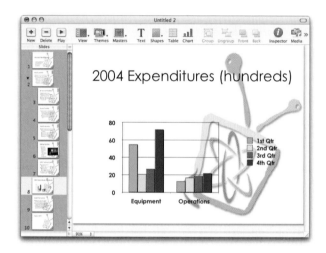

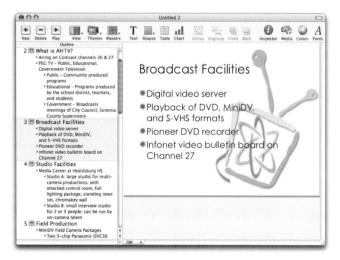

The Outline view replaces the slide thumbnails with the text on the slides, making it easier for you to work with the text without distraction.

The Slide Only view (not shown) hides the Slide Navigator, Outline, and speaker notes.

anatomy of a slide

To make it easier to create your slides, Keynote provides placeholders on its slides, into which you can put text, graphics, or charts. These placeholders are arranged into preset slide masters, and every slide in your presentation is based on one of these masters. Besides the slide master, each presentation also has a single theme, which provides the visual look of the slide, including things like the background image for the slides and the style and color of the text you put on the slides.

Slide masters with slots for graphics, charts, or movies come with Placeholders that tell you where to add the object. The photo cutouts on this slide allowed me to drop in two photos from my iPhoto library.

The Background is an image that is part of the theme.

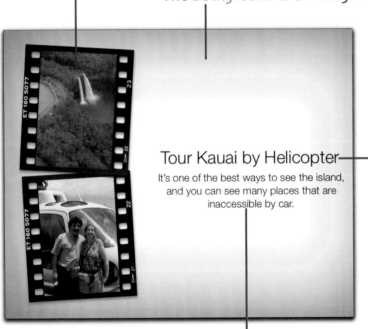

Tour Kauai by Helicopter

It's one of the best ways to see the island, and you can see many places that are inaccessible by car.

A Title is included on each slide master (except for the Blank master). The title corresponds to the main heading for each slide in the presentation's outline. You'll learn more about outlines in Chapter 2.

A slide's Body Text is contained in one or more text boxes. The body text can be bulleted or numbered lists, a caption for an image, or plain text.

save the presentation

Save your presentation file before you continue to the next chapter. Choose File > Save, or press Cmd-S.

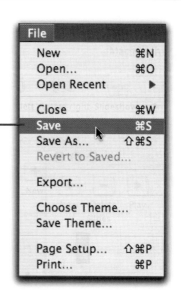

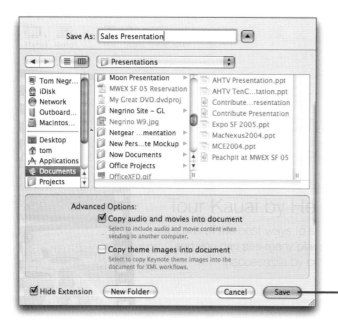

The first time you save, the Save As box appears. This is where you name the presentation. Type the name you want in the Save As box, then click the Save button.

extra bits

keynote main window p. 2

- Your speaker Notes will appear on your laptop screen during your presentation if you are using a PowerBook, which has the ability to use multiple monitors, where the laptop screen shows something differently than the external projector or monitor. If your laptop is an iBook, you won't be able to see speaker Notes, because iBooks are only capable of monitor mirroring, in which the laptop and external screens are identical.

explore the toolbar p. 3

- You can customize the toolbar by choosing View > Customize Toolbar, which brings up a dialog that has all of the possible toolbar buttons. You can add or subtract buttons from the toolbar to suit your style of work.

- You can Control-click (or right-click if you have a mouse with multiple buttons) on the toolbar to bring up a shortcut menu that allows you to view the toolbar buttons as just Icons, Icons and Text (the default), or just Text. The shortcut menu also has an option to use smaller icons for the toolbar buttons.

explore the inspector p. 5

- You're not limited to just one Inspector window; you can have multiple Inspector windows on the screen by choosing View > New Inspector. If you have the screen real estate, it's a good way to keep all of the tools you want near at hand.

anatomy of a slide p. 9

- You can add slide numbers to your presentation by turning them on in the Appearance tab of the Slide Inspector.

save the presentation p. 10

- You will find it useful to save all of the files used in the project in a single folder you create inside your Documents folder. That way, everything you need for the presentation is in one place. I suggest that you name the folder with the name of your presentation or with the name of the venue or event. For example, I have a Presentations folder in my Documents folder. Inside that, I create one additional folder for each presentation I do, labeled by the name of the event at which I am speaking. The key is to give the folder a name that will allow you to find a particular presentation easily.

2. write your presentation

Now that you've created your presentation file, you need to write the presentation. And the best place to write the presentation is not on the slides, but in Keynote's Outline View. Now, it's possible that, like many of us, you were scared off of outlines by your sixth grade teacher. You should reconsider, because Outline View is Keynote's secret weapon for making better presentations. When you write in the outline, you can focus on the content of your presentation, rather than getting distracted by the look of the presentation. Text that you write in the Outline pane will also appear on your slides, and vice versa.

We've all seen presentations where the presenter spent more time on the appearance than the message. But your message is the most important part of your presentation. The biggest trap of presentation software is seducing you with flashy pictures, distracting you from your message. By writing the presentation in the outline before you even consider the look, you'll avoid that pitfall—and you'll be way ahead of most other presenters.

You don't need to do anything extra to get an outline; every presentation has an outline underneath, so it makes sense to start in the outline, rather than on the slide.

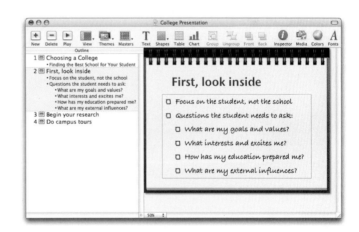

write the outline

Switch to Outline View by choosing View > Outline, or by choosing Outline from the View pop-up menu in the toolbar.

When Outline View becomes active, the Outline pane becomes bigger, to make room for you to work, but you can still see a preview of the slide in the Slide pane. If you need even more room in the outline, point at the handle at the bottom of the window, between the Outline pane and the Slide pane, and when the cursor becomes a double-headed arrow, drag the border so the pane is as wide as you want.

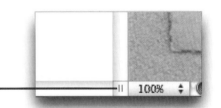

The first slide is a Title slide, which contains the title and subtitle for the presentation. The first line, or heading, in your outline is the title of your presentation. In the outline, click in the top line to place the insertion point, type the title, then press Return.

Hey, what's this? Keynote created a new slide, rather than letting you type the subtitle on the first slide.

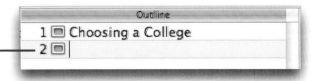

write your presentation

No problem; press the Tab key. That tells Keynote that you want to create a subheading, which is a heading indented below an existing heading.

You can see from the slide preview that your slide is looking the way that you want.

You're done for now with the Title slide (we'll dress it up with graphics in later chapters), so choose Slide > New Slide, or click the New button on the toolbar. Keynote creates the new slide, and automatically assigns it the Title and Bullets layout.

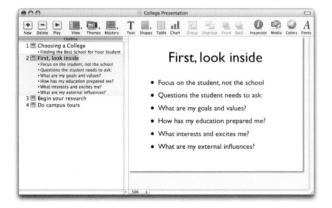

Type the title of the second slide, press Return, then press Tab and type the bullet points for your second slide, pressing Return between each bullet point. As you type, the slide preview updates. When you're done with the slide, press Return, then press Shift-Tab to get a new slide. Continue for the rest of your presentation.

write your presentation

work with outline text

The flexibility of Keynote's Outline View is that it makes it easy to rearrange your ideas as you work on your presentation. Let's look at the outline for the last slide we wrote:

2 ▣ First, look inside
- Focus on the student, not the school
- Questions the student needs to ask:
- What are my goals and values?
- How has my education prepared me?
- What interests and excites me?
- What are my external influences?

It's okay, but it needs better organization. Some headings can move up and others would be better as subheadings. To move headings around, you will drag bullets with the mouse or use keyboard shortcuts. To select a bullet and its text, click on the bullet, which will highlight the text.

2 ▣ First, look inside
- Focus on the student, not the school
- Questions the student needs to ask:
- What are my goals and values?
- How has my education prepared me?
- What interests and excites me?
- What are my external influences?

Click and drag the bullet to move the heading and any subheads up or down in the outline. You can select more than one bullet at a time: click on the first bullet, hold down the Shift key, and click the last bullet. All bullets in between will highlight.

To move one or more headings right, making them a lower level of subhead, select the bullet, then press Tab, or drag the bullet until a blue triangle appears, showing you the level the heading will move to. When you release the mouse button, the headings move to the lower level.

2 ▣ First, look inside
- Focus on the student, not the school
- Questions the student needs to ask:
- What are my goals and values?
- What interests and excites me?
- How has my education prepared me?
- What are my external influences?

write your presentation

To move one or more headings left, making them a higher outline level, select the heading, then press Shift-Tab, or drag them left with the mouse until you see the blue triangle.

After a few strategic moves, the outline is better organized.

Outline

These headings became subheads.

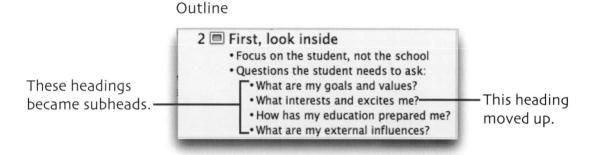

This heading moved up.

Slide

First, look inside

- Focus on the student, not the school
- Questions the student needs to ask:
  - What are my goals and values?
  - What interests and excites me?
  - How has my education prepared me?
  - What are my external influences?

use OmniOutliner

If you want an outline program with more features than Keynote's Outline View, you can turn to The Omni Group's OmniOutliner (www.omnigroup.com/applications/omnioutliner/), which makes it easier to produce outlines. And you can export an OmniOutliner document as a Keynote presentation, which saves you time.

OmniOutliner is a commercial product, but you can download a free trial version. Or you may already have the program and not know it; it is part of the software bundle included on PowerBooks and the Power Mac G5.

You can write the outline and move headings around in much the same way that you can in Keynote, but OmniOutliner gives you many options for reorganizing, sorting, formatting, and zooming in to parts of the outline.

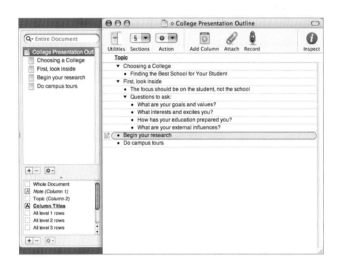

Once you have written your outline in OmniOutliner, choose File > Export, then choose Apple Keynote 2 from the File Format pop-up menu. Click Save, and OmniOutliner exports the outline as a Keynote presentation file.

Back in Keynote, choose File > Open, select the presentation file, and click Open.

write your presentation

extra bits

write the outline p. 14

- If the text in the outline is too small to work with comfortably, you can change it by choosing Keynote > Preferences, then clicking the General button in the toolbar of the Preferences window. At the bottom of the window, pick the font and font size you want from the Outline View Font pop-up menu.

use OmniOutliner p. 18

- If you're dealing with a large presentation, you have a large outline. And OmniOutliner, being a full-fledged outline processor, has better tools for working with larger outlines. For example, you have more control over the number of heading levels that you show or hide at any given time, which lets you concentrate on the points that are important without being distracted by supporting information.

- If you often use a particular design theme in Keynote, you can choose it in OmniOutliner's Preferences so that you don't have to change themes or reformat once you open the exported OmniOutliner presentation in Keynote.

work with outline text p. 16

- You can move bullets from one slide to another by dragging them out of the current slide to a different slide.

- If you drag a bullet to the left of the other bullets on a slide until a blue triangle appears above the slide, you will create a new slide containing that bullet.

- You can click and drag on a slide icon to move the slide and its contents up or down in your presentation.

- If you double-click a slide icon in Outline View, it will hide its bulleted text, showing only the slide's title. This is often useful when you are rearranging slides.

- You can also print the outline: choose File > Print, choose Keynote from the resulting Print dialog's Copies and Pages pop-up menu, choose Outline, and click Print.

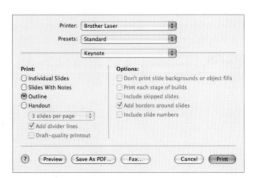

3. gather image and sound files

Now that you've written your presentation outline, I'll let you in on a secret; the hardest part of creating your presentation is behind you. From this point, you're adding more elements to the presentation to add impact to the story you're telling and making the slides look good. But before we plunge into the nitty-gritty of changing the look of your slides, there's still one more important bit of planning to do. You need to decide which parts of your presentation's message will be enhanced with the addition of pictures and media files such as sounds and video. We've all seen presentations where the speaker threw in pictures and sounds seemingly at random, and that tends to turn audiences off. A quick review of your slides helps you avoid this pitfall.

In this chapter, we'll figure out where images, sounds, and even video clips could enhance your presentation, find images, and talk a bit about using sound in Keynote slideshows.

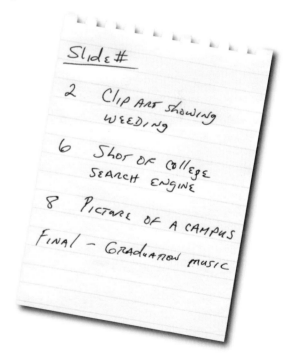

Slide #

2   Clip Art showing weeding

6   Shot of college search engine

8   Picture of a campus

Final — Graduation music

review your slides

For the first time, we're going to look at material on the slides, rather than in the outline, with an eye to deciding where we want to add images or sounds. You'll need a notepad or scratch paper to take notes as you browse the slides.

Switch to the Slide Navigator by choosing Navigator from the View pop-up menu on the toolbar, or choose View > Navigator. The slide thumbnails appear.

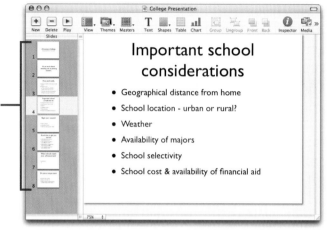

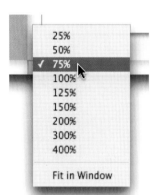

If the Notes pane is showing and you want to see a bigger view of the slide, choose View > Hide Notes. You can also use the Zoom menu at the bottom of the window to resize the slide within the Slide pane.

Click on slides in the Slide Navigator to browse through your slides (you can also use the Up or Down Arrow keys on your keyboard to move through your slides). As you re-read the contents of each slide, think about what pictures you could add to the slide that would help your audience better grasp your message. Some slides won't need any help from images; others will benefit from an added image. For example, on the slide in my presentation about the campus visit, a picture of a college campus would be helpful, because it would add visual interest.

As you browse, jot down notes with the slide number and what sort of image, sound file, or even video clip you could add that would enhance the slide.

gather image and sound files

view the master slides

Now that you know what sorts of images you might want to use, it's time to start thinking about how those images will appear on your slides. You'll do this by looking at the master slides that Keynote provides. Master slides are part of the presentation's theme, which you selected back in Chapter 1 when you created the presentation (you chose the plain White theme). Themes can contain any number of master slides, depending on what the theme designer chose to include. The themes created by Apple that come with Keynote contain between 11 and 17 master slides, for instance. When you create a new slide in your presentation, Keynote copies one of the master slides, and the objects (text boxes, pictures, tables, or charts) from the master slide are placed on the new slide.

There are two ways to view the master slides in the current theme. If you choose the Masters pop-up menu on the toolbar, you get a nice menu of the master slides available in the theme.

view the master slides

You can also choose View > Show Master Slides. This splits the Slide Navigator into two panes, with the master slides in the top pane, and your presentation slides in the bottom pane.

In either view, the slide masters appear with their names and thumbnails, so it's easy to tell master slides apart and quick to choose the one you want.

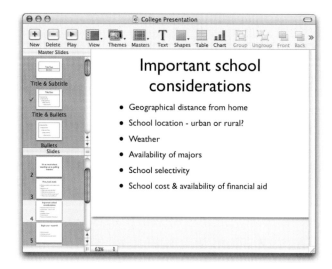

As you browse through the slide masters, you can see how a slide will look with that master applied by first displaying the slide, then choosing the master by selecting it in the Masters pop-up menu or clicking it in the Master Slides section of the Slide Navigator, then dragging the master onto the slide you're viewing in the Slides pane. The slide will change to match the new slide master's layout, and, if necessary, it will reformat the slide's text.

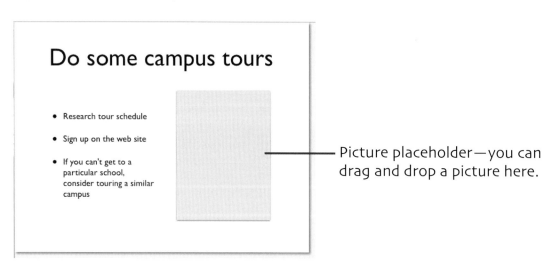

Picture placeholder—you can drag and drop a picture here.

gather image and sound files

find images

Images you use in your presentations can come from many possible sources: digital pictures you take yourself; scanned photographs or drawings; stock photography that you purchase online; or clip art. There are some very fine clip art packages available; see the extra bits for this chapter for more details.

There are two excellent sources of clip art that may not immediately come to mind, and they are both available to you if you own Microsoft Office. One is the built-in Office clip art library. You can find it by launching Microsoft Word and choosing Insert > Picture > Clip Art. This opens the Clip Gallery.

To search the clip art, enter a word in the Search field, and then click Search.

You'll add images to your slides in Chapter 6. For now, look through the available images in the clip art collections to find images that you may want to use. As you browse the clip art, take notes on images that might be useful.

If you're not happy with the selection of clip art that comes with Microsoft Office, there's a lot more available for free at Microsoft Office Online, at http://office.Microsoft.com/clipart/.

If you find suitable images among the vast collection on Microsoft Office Online, download them to your local machine for later use.

pick sounds or video

Finding sounds or video for your presentation is a bit trickier than finding images. Most video you use will be video that you shoot yourself. If you do have video, add it to the Movies folder on your hard disk, and it will be available in Keynote in the Movies pane of the Media palette.

There are two categories of sounds that you can use in your presentations: sound effects, which are usually short sound clips that you use to punctuate a point, and music.

You can find sound effects on the Web; there are many Web sites that sell royalty-free sound collections, such as SoundRangers (www.soundrangers.com). These sites sell individual sounds for as little as $1.50. You'll find more sites with a Google search on "sounds" "royalty-free". Most of these sites allow you to download sound effects in MP3 format, which opens in iTunes.

The best way to deal with music you want to use in the presentation is to import it into iTunes. You can then use it directly in Keynote using the Music pane of the Media palette.

You'll add sounds and video to slides in Chapter 6. For now, make note of the sounds that would work with your presentation.

gather image and sound files

extra bits

review your slides p. 22

- The Zoom menu at the bottom of the Keynote window just changes the view of the slide on your screen; it doesn't change the size of elements on the slide itself.

- Use the Fit In Window choice in the Zoom menu to have the slide automatically resize as you change the size of the Keynote window.

view the master slides p. 23

- When you choose View > Show Master Slides and the Slide Navigator splits into the Master Slides and Slides panes, you can adjust the size of the two panes by dragging the handle in the border between the two panes.

find images p. 25

- Images you use in your presentations should be royalty free, meaning they can be used without additional payments to the image's producer.

- Clip art and other media found at the Microsoft Office Online site are subject to certain restrictions, which are listed at the site. At the bottom of the clip art page, you'll find a link called "Legal." Click it, and be prepared to be stunned into submission by legal-eze.

- There are many places online to find images for your presentations. Rather than try to single out just a few companies, do a Google search on all of the following search terms: "images" "royalty-free" "clip art". You'll get a wealth of choices, some free, some not.

- Besides online resources, you can find many excellent clip art packages on the market. These come on CD or DVD, and are usually royalty free. Some good ones are from Hemera (www.hemera.com), in their Photo-Objects collections, and Nova Development's Art Explosion series (www.novadevelopment.com). Digital Juice (www.digitaljuice.com) has the Presenter's Toolkit package, which contains thousands of images, video clips, animations, and backgrounds.

extra bits

pick sounds or video p. 26

- If you're musically inclined (or even if you're not), and if you have iLife, you can use GarageBand to create music for your presentations. Create a soundtrack using GarageBand's built-in music loops, export it to iTunes, and it will show up in the Media palette. If you need help using GarageBand, let me suggest GarageBand 2 for Mac OS X: Visual QuickStart Guide, by Victor Gavenda, or Take Control of Making Music with GarageBand, an e-book by Jeff Tolbert (www.tidbits.com/takecontrol/).

- Microsoft Office for Mac's Clip Gallery doesn't come with sounds, but you can add sounds to the Clip Gallery—it's a convenient place to store them.

4. pick a theme

With your presentation's content set, it's time to start dressing up your slides. You'll do that in this chapter by selecting a theme for your presentation. Themes are templates that provide the visual look of the slides throughout the whole presentation, including elements like a background image for the slides and the style and color of the text you put on the slides. Themes also control the look of other slide elements, such as charts and tables.

You'll also apply a master slide to each slide in your presentation, matching the layout to the content of the slide. For example, you'll apply the Title & Subtitle layout to the first slide, and add a layout that contains image placeholders for slides where you will add pictures.

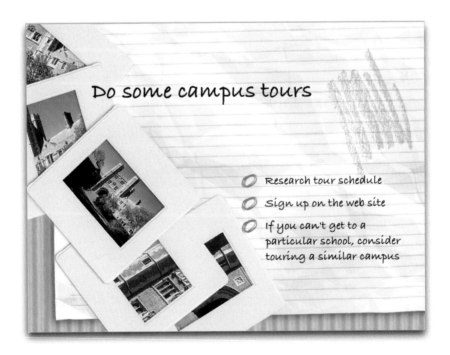

choose your theme

When you pick a theme, Keynote applies it to all of the slides in the presentation, so that all of the slides will have a consistent look.

Begin applying a theme by clicking one of the slides in the Slide Navigator to display one of the presentation's slides. Any slide will do, but I usually use a slide that contains a title and bulleted text, because those are the most common in presentations.

To pick one of the available themes, choose File > Choose Theme. The Theme Chooser dialog appears.

Each theme appears as a thumbnail preview, and the current theme is outlined in yellow. Scroll through the dialog until you find a theme you like. Click the thumbnail of the theme, and choose from the two pop-up menus. The Apply Theme To menu allows you to apply the theme to all of the slides or just slides you have selected in the Slide Navigator. In this case, choose All Slides. The choices available from the Slide Size menu depend on the theme you have chosen. All of the themes Apple supplies with Keynote, and virtually all third-party themes, come in both 800 x 600 or 1024 x 768 pixel sizes.

Selected theme

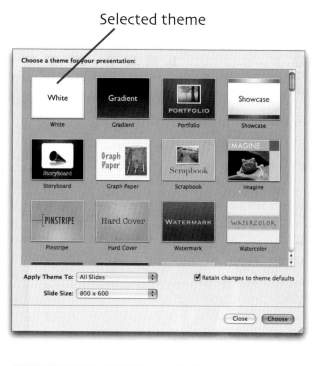

Some third-party themes have additional sizes, such as themes designed to fill a wide-screen monitor. Click the Choose button to apply the theme to your presentation.

pick a theme

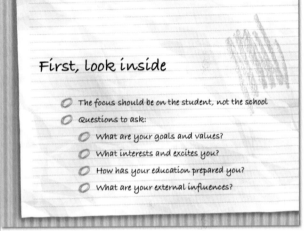

You can see how applying the slide design has changed the font and styles of the text on the slide; the positioning of the text on the slide; the slide's background image; and the style of the bullets used on the slide (from dots to circles).

apply master slides

Now it's time to go through all of your slides and apply the proper master slide to each one.

In the Slide Navigator, scroll to the first slide in your presentation, which is the title slide. The slide should be using the Title & Subtitle or Title – Center layout. If it is not (it usually isn't if you imported the slide outline from another application, for example), choose the slide master you want from the Masters pop-up menu in the toolbar.

The slide changes to match the layout of the slide master.

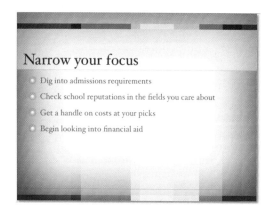

Slide with Title & Bullets master

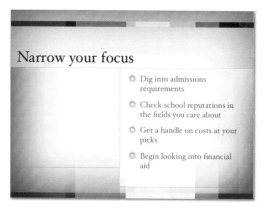

Slide with Title & Bullets - Right master

Use the Slide Navigator to move through your slides, applying appropriate layouts to each one. This is where the notes you took in Chapter 3 will come in handy; because you've already figured out where images will go in your presentation, you can apply picture layouts where it is appropriate.

pick a theme

modify master slides

Most of the time, you'll probably like the styles and layouts in the master slides from the theme that you are using. But each presentation is different, and sometimes you want to change one or more of the master slides to better fit the content of your presentation. You'll do this by making changes to master slides in the presentation. Of course, if you're happy with the master slides that come with the theme, you can skip this step.

Note that modifying a master slide changes it only for the presentation file you are currently working in; it doesn't modify the copy of the master slide that is in the theme file.

If you want to change elements on the master slide such as text boxes, tables, or graphics, begin by choosing View > Show Master Slides. The Slide Navigator will split to show the master slides in the current presentation.

In this example, we'll change the background for a master slide. In the future, applying that master slide will create a slide with the alternate background. When creating custom master slides, it's best to take an existing master slide, duplicate it, and then change the duplicate. Scroll through the list of master slides until you find the Title - Top master, then click to select it. Next, choose Edit > Duplicate. You will get a new master slide named Title - Top copy. Rename the master slide by selecting its name and typing a new name. I named my new master slide Alt Background.

modify master slides (cont.)

In the Inspector, click the Master Slide button in the toolbar, then click the Appearance tab.

You need to pick an image file for the new background. In the background section of the Master Slide Inspector, click the Choose button. This brings up an Open dialog. Find and select the image you want to use for the new background, then click Open. The slide will change to reflect the new background.

Master Slide Inspector button

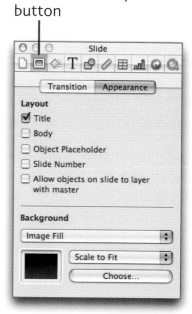

To use your new master slide, choose View > Hide Master Slides. Then click the New button on the toolbar to create a new slide. Choose the new Alt Background layout from the Masters pop-up menu in the toolbar.

pick a theme

The slide master is applied to the slide you just created, with the new background as you added it.

Getting the most from a campus visit

- Be there at the right time
- Ask lots of questions – and to the right people
- Campus stats – handle with care
- Try it yourself – classes, food, and more
- If you can, stay overnight
- Make notes about each school

pick a theme

adjust slide elements

After applying the slide design and possibly customizing the background, you may find that some of the text on your slides isn't quite where you want it. For example, the title slide of my presentation had the placeholder containing the subtitle overlapping the line separating the title and subtitle, and the title is too close to the line, too.

The text on the slide is in placeholders, and you can move the placeholders as you like.

Click once on the text in a text box to select the text box. The handles will appear at the edges of the box.

You can drag the text box as you like. Clicking and dragging any of the text box's selection handles resizes the text box.

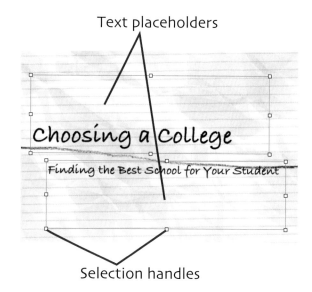

Text placeholders

Selection handles

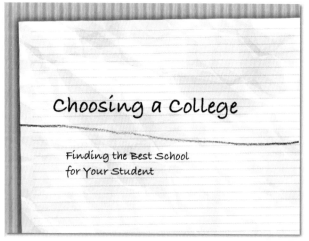

After the text boxes are moved around, the slide looks better.

extra bits

choose your theme p. 30

- You can also bring up the Theme Chooser by picking it from the Themes pop-up menu in the toolbar.

- Keynote 2 adds the ability to have slides with different themes in a single presentation. This is both good and bad. It's good because you can now vary your theme as you wish in a presentation for a special effect. But if you are trying out a variety of themes to see what they are like with your presentation, it's bad, because every time you change themes, all of the master slides for each theme you try get copied into your presentation file. You can end up with dozens of unneeded and unused master slides in your presentation, and this can slow down the program.

  One workaround, if you want to preview lots of themes, is to copy and paste a few representative slides from your presentation into a new Keynote file, then use that new file to experiment. For example, you could copy the title slide, a slide using the Title & Bullets master, and a slide using the Title, Bullets & Photo master into a new presentation file. Then try out different themes in the new

file. When you find a theme that you like, simply close the file you're using for experimentation without saving it. Then return to your real presentation and apply only the theme you prefer.

- You can apply a master slide by dragging it from the Master Slides pane onto a slide in the Slides pane. This even works between two different Keynote documents; it's a good way to copy a master slide from one presentation to another without importing the whole theme.

- By default, Keynote shows you the Theme Chooser dialog whenever you create a new Keynote document. If you prefer, you can instead have Keynote always default to a particular theme. Just choose Keynote > Preferences, then click the General button.

continues on next page

---

pick a theme

extra bits

In the For New Documents section, click Use theme, then click the Choose button. The Theme Chooser dialog will appear. Choose the theme and the slide size you want, then click the Choose button. The Theme Chooser dialog will close and the name of the theme you selected will appear in the Preferences window.

- For the college presentation I'm creating, I've chosen a third-party theme called Education Pro, created by Jumsoft (www. jumsoft.com/themes/).

apply master slides p. 32

- Want more choices than the themes that come with Keynote? There are many places to find more themes on the Web. I've listed some of the best sites at the companion site for this book, at www.negrino.com/keynote-vqj/.

modify master slides p. 33

- Keynote can use just about any graphic file (in a standard format such as JPEG, TIFF, or PNG) as a slide background. To make a new background, you'll need a graphic editing program, such as Adobe Photoshop or Macromedia Fireworks. Those

programs are terrific, but they're not cheap, and you can get by with less expensive alternatives. The shareware GraphicConverter (www.lemkesoft.com) is a good choice.

- You can use any item in the iPhoto section of the Media Browser as the source for a master slide background.

- Just as there are sites that sell themes, others sell slide backgrounds. One of my favorites is PowerPoint Art (www. powerpointart.com), which sells a subscription that allows you to use any of their thousands of backgrounds. Don't worry that the site is focused on PowerPoint; the files will work just fine in Keynote. A Google search will turn up many other sites that sell slide backgrounds.

adjust slide elements p. 36

- You can often make your slides look even better by changing the font size or text alignment. You'll see how to do that in Chapter 5.

5. work with text

Even though you've done most of the writing of your presentation in the outline, now that you see the text on the slides with your preferred slide design, you will probably want to make some changes on the slides themselves.

In this chapter, you'll learn how to edit and format text on the slides, add hyperlinks (a new feature in Keynote 2), and even add extra text to a slide for special purposes like adding captions to images. Finally, you'll learn how to avoid a major presentation embarrassment: misspellings on your slides.

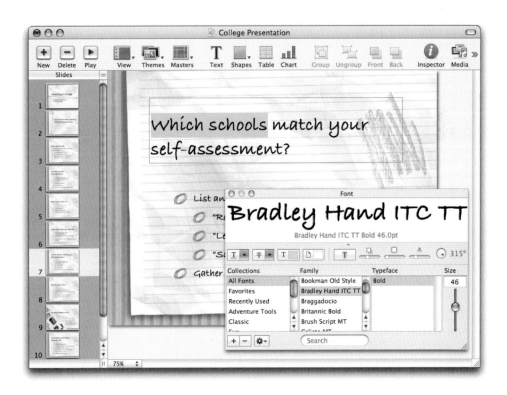

edit slide text

If you want to change or add text to a slide, move the mouse pointer over the text and click once to select the text box, and then click once again to set the insertion point. The cursor will change into a blinking vertical line, indicating where you can start typing.

Text box ——

Narrow your focus

Insertion point cursor

Type to add or delete text. You can also use the insertion point cursor to select text inside a text box. Click and drag over the text you want to select. Once it is selected, you can type to replace the selected text.

Selected text

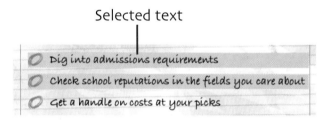

Dig into admissions requirements

Check school reputations in the fields you care about

Get a handle on costs at your picks

work with text

The most common reason to want to edit text on a slide (besides changing the words to better convey your meaning) is to make the text work better with your slide design, which usually means getting a line of text to break in a different spot. A line break is the point on a line at which the text wraps down to the next line.

For example, let's look again at the title slide of my presentation. Originally, the subtitle and my name and title were in long lines, which didn't look that great.

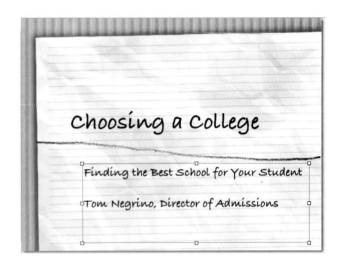

To change the text so that it wraps more attractively, we'll add manual line breaks to the text. Click to set the insertion point before the word where you want the break to happen.

You can't just press Return, because Keynote will think that you want to create a new paragraph, which on slides with bulleted text will result in a new bullet point. Instead, press Shift-Return, which adds a line break without adding a paragraph break. On the next line, I deleted the comma after my name and added a manual line break. The result is considerably more pleasing to the eye.

format slide text

Another way to change the text on your slides is to change its formatting, including the size and look of the text, alignment, and spacing between the lines.

You'll make most text changes the way you would in a word processor. First you select the text, and then make choices from the Fonts or Colors window, the Inspector, or the menu bar, depending on what you want to accomplish. To open the Inspector, or the Fonts or Colors window, click its button on the toolbar.

To change font or font size, you use the Fonts window (page 43).

To change text color (or the colors for any Keynote object), you use the Colors window (page 44).

To quickly add bold or italic to text, select the text and choose either Format > Font > Bold or Format > Font > Italic.

For example, let's say that you want to emphasize some text on one of your slides. First, click and drag to select the text.

Then make your choice from the menu bar.

Demo Time!

Demo Time!

Fonts window

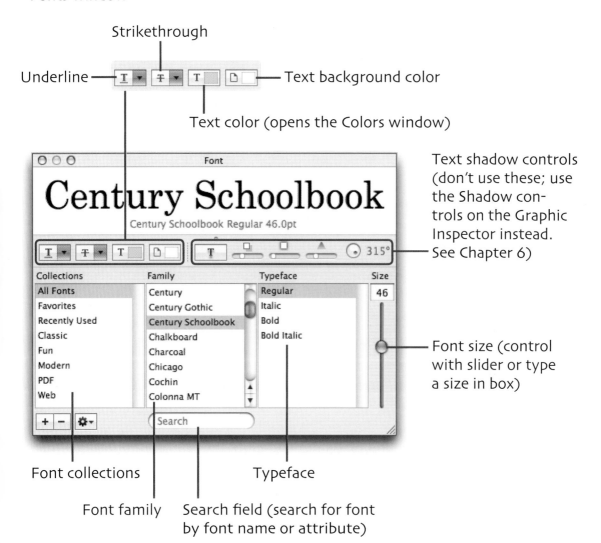

Strikethrough

Underline

Text background color

Text color (opens the Colors window)

Text shadow controls (don't use these; use the Shadow controls on the Graphic Inspector instead. See Chapter 6)

Century Schoolbook

Century Schoolbook Regular 46.0pt

315°

Collections	Family	Typeface	Size
All Fonts	Century	Regular	46
Favorites	Century Gothic	Italic	
Recently Used	Century Schoolbook	Bold	
Classic	Chalkboard	Bold Italic	
Fun	Charcoal		
Modern	Chicago		
PDF	Cochin		
Web	Colonna MT		

Search

Font size (control with slider or type a size in box)

Font collections

Typeface

Font family

Search field (search for font by font name or attribute)

format slide text (cont.)

Colors window

Click in this toolbar to view different types of color pickers.

Click the magnifying glass to pick up a color anywhere on the screen (it works like the eyedropper in most other graphic programs).

Click to select a color in the color wheel.

Drag colors from the color well to save them for later use in the color palette.

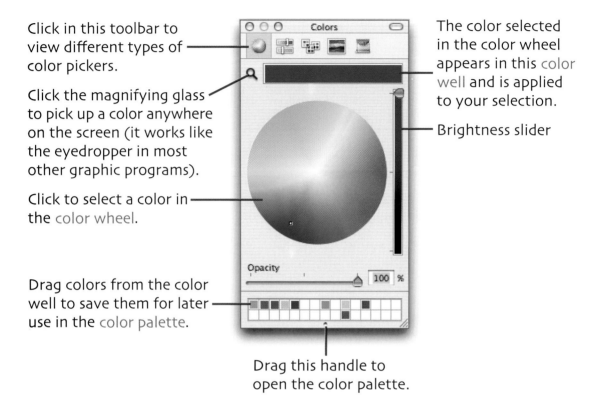

The color selected in the color wheel appears in this color well and is applied to your selection.

Brightness slider

Drag this handle to open the color palette.

align slide text

When you're working with graphics, you may want to change text alignment in text boxes so that they work better with the image. Or you may decide that left-aligned or right-aligned text looks better on your title slide, instead of the center alignment that is the setting on most design templates.

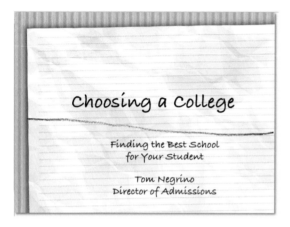

Center-aligned text

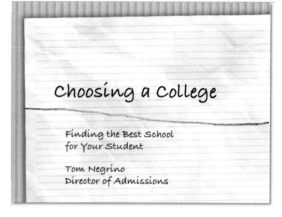

Left-aligned text

align slide text (cont.)

To set text alignment, open the Inspector (if it isn't already open) by clicking the Inspector button on the toolbar. Then click the Text Inspector button on the Inspector toolbar. In the Color & Alignment section of the Text tab, you'll find the alignment controls. Select the text, then click one of the text alignment buttons.

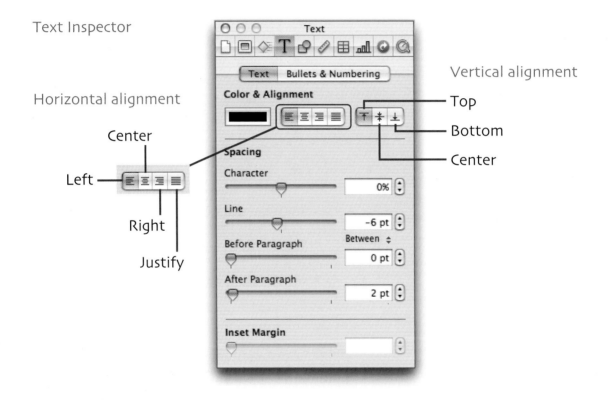

Text Inspector

Horizontal alignment

Center

Left

Right

Justify

Vertical alignment

Top

Bottom

Center

change line spacing

You can spread the line spacing on a slide if it is too tight for the content, or reduce the line spacing if you need to get a little more text on the slide.

On this slide, the indented text would be easier to read if the lines were a bit further apart.

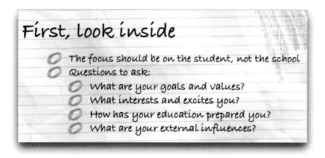

Select all of the lines of indented text, then open the Text Inspector.

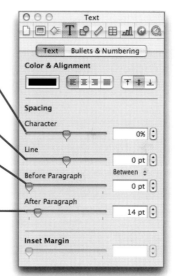

Use this to change the amount of space between characters. This is usually useful for titles and special effects, rather than bulleted text.

Use this to change the line spacing.

Use this to change the amount of space before each paragraph.

Use this to change the amount of space after each paragraph.

As you use the spacing controls, the slide text changes to reflect your new line spacing.

use numbered lists

Bulleted lists are standard in presentations, but sometimes you want to show a process with a clear beginning and end. For that, a numbered list is better. You can easily change the bulleted lists that Keynote gives you into a numbered list, and customize the numbering as you wish.

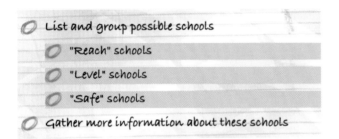

First, select the bulleted text.

Open the Text Inspector, and click on the Bullets & Numbering tab.

From the style pop-up menu, choose Numbers. The text changes to a numbered list. If you want a different numbering system (maybe you would prefer letters rather than numbers, i.e., A, B, C...), choose it from the number style pop-up menu.

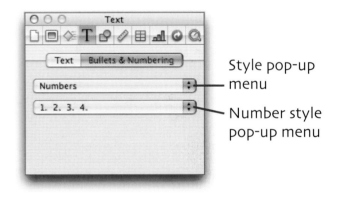

Style pop-up menu

Number style pop-up menu

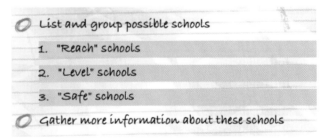

work with text

customize bullets

Many themes have alternate bullets that you can use to dress up your slides. And you may want to use a different style of bullet to emphasize some of your points. Just be careful to use alternate bullets tastefully and appropriately; too many different styles will annoy your audience.

To change the bullet style, first select the bulleted text.

Open the Text Inspector, and click on the Bullets & Numbering tab.

From the style pop-up menu, choose Image Bullets. In the scrollable list of bullet styles, find the one you want to use, then select it.

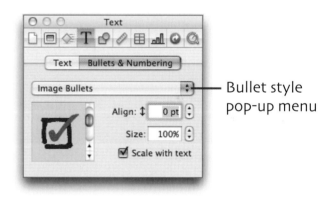

Bullet style pop-up menu

The bullets change to your selected style.

customize bullets (cont.)

Besides image bullets, you can also use text bullets by choosing Text Bullets from the style menu. This gives you a pop-up menu with bullets from which to choose, and a color well so you can change the bullet color. Click in the color well to bring up the Colors window, then adjust the bullet color.

Text bullet pop-up menu —

Color well —

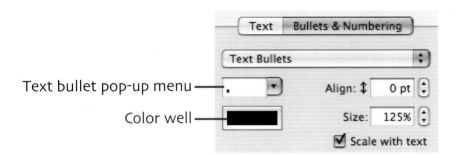

add hyperlinks

You're already familiar with hyperlinks; they're the underlined text that you click in a Web browser that takes you to another Web page. You can use two kinds of hyperlinks in your Keynote presentations. The first kind, when clicked during your presentation, leaves Keynote and hides it, opens the default Web browser on your machine, and brings you to the hyperlink's destination. The other kind of hyperlink makes Keynote jump to a different slide in your presentation. Either kind of hyperlink only works while you are actually presenting; you don't have to worry about accidentally opening your Web browser while you are working on your presentation.

If you type a Web address into the outline or a Keynote slide—such as www.peachpit.com—Keynote is smart enough to automatically turn it into a hyperlink. In many instances, that's all you'll need, because the link shows your audience the Web address you want them to use and also allows you to click it to display the site.

Good sites to get you started

- www.universities.com
- www.collegeview.com
- www.review.com/college
- www.collegeboard.org

add hyperlinks (cont.)

If you want text on your slide to be the link instead, follow these steps:

1 Select the text that you want to make into a hyperlink.

2 Open the Inspector, then click the button for the Hyperlink Inspector.

3 Click the Enable as a hyperlink checkbox.

4 From the Link To pop-up menu, choose Webpage.

5 In the URL field, type the full Web address for the hyperlink. You don't have to add the http:// before the address; Keynote will add it automatically when you leave the URL field. The text is underlined, indicating that it has become a hyperlink.

To make the other kind of hyperlink—the kind that jumps to a different slide in your presentation—follow these steps:

1 Select the text you want to use as the hyperlink.

2 In the Hyperlink Inspector, click the Enable as a hyperlink checkbox.

3 From the Link To pop-up menu, choose Slide.

4 Make a choice from the options that appear.

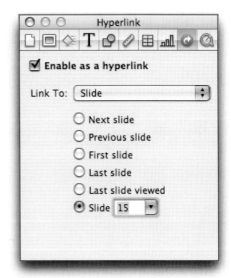

work with text

add text boxes

There are many reasons why you might want text on your slides that isn't part of the outline, but the most common reason is to add text that will be a label or caption for a picture, table, or chart. To add this text, you'll first need to add a text box to the slide.

Choose Insert > Text. A text box appears on the slide, with the placeholder text Text.

Click and drag the new text box to place it where you want it on the slide. Double click the placeholder text, then type the text you want in the new text box. The text box automatically resizes to contain the text you enter.

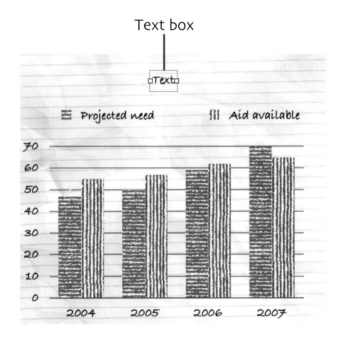

After you create the text box, you can apply any formatting you like to the text it contains, using the Inspector, Fonts, or Colors palette.

check your spelling

Aside from those dreams that you had when you were a kid that you were naked in front of your geometry class (uh, maybe that was just me), there's nothing much more embarrassing than doing a presentation with a misspelled word. Your mistake is there for everyone to see, and it's projected 10 feet wide, to boot! Avoid this nightmare by using Keynote's spelling tools.

The nice thing is that Keynote is always watching you like a hawk as you write, looking for spelling mistakes. If it finds one, it puts a dotted red underline under the suspected mistake. To fix it, Control-click (or right-click if you have a mouse with multiple buttons) the word. You'll get a shortcut menu with one or more suggested corrections.

Choose the correction you want from the menu, and Keynote replaces the misspelling.

You can also check spelling throughout your whole presentation. Choose Edit > Spelling > Spelling. The Spelling dialog appears, and finds the first questionable word.

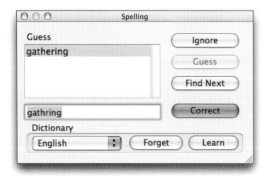

In the Guess list, click the correct spelling, then click the Correct button. If the word is correct (just not in Keynote's dictionary), click Ignore. If you want to add the word to the system-wide dictionary, click the Learn button. Close the Spelling dialog when no more misspelled words are found.

extra bits

edit slide text p. 40

- Double-clicking on a word on a slide selects that word; triple-clicking selects the entire line.
- Keynote lacks a handy feature you might have used in Power-Point. Keynote doesn't automatically resize text and reduce line spacing in order to fit too-long text within text boxes. You'll have to manage the fit of your text within text boxes manually. On the other hand, this keeps you from squeezing too much text on your slides; text heavy slides are hard for the audience to digest.
- Despite what it says on the slide, I am not the Director of Admissions for any college or university, and I can't help your kid get into college. But as I write this, my wife and I are working on getting our son into a good school, so this presentation topic is near and dear to our hearts.

format slide text p. 42

- When you want to emphasize text, use italic, rather than underline. People tend to interpret underlined text as a Web link.

- When you italicize text, Keynote uses the italic version of the font the text is using. If that font doesn't have an italic version, choosing Format > Font > Italic won't appear to do anything. Bold works in a similar fashion. You can see if a font has an italic (or bold) version in the Typeface section of the Fonts window.
- If you have applied multiple formatting changes to text and you want to make the same changes to other text, you don't have to make all those formatting changes again. Instead, copy and paste the text format. First, select the text that has the formatting you want to copy. Then choose Format > Copy Style, or press Command-Option-C. Then select the text you want to style in the same way and choose Format > Paste Style, or press Command-Option-V.
- If you make too many changes and decide you don't want any of them, it's easy to revert back to the formatting from the master slide. Just select whatever you want to change back and choose Format > Reapply Master to Selection.

extra bits

align slide text p. 45

- Sometime it's better to move a text placeholder on the slide, rather than mess with text alignment. See "adjust slide elements" in Chapter 4 for more information.

use numbered lists p. 48

- If you are familiar with Power-Point, you know you can change the starting number of the list, which is handy when you're continuing a list from a previous slide. Unfortunately, you cannot do this in Keynote.

- When you choose a numbering system, pick one that matches the flavor of your presentation. For example, in a formal presentation, you might want to consider using Roman numerals as the numbering system. But that would probably be inappropriate (not to mention pompous) in a presentation about softball teams. Whatever you choose, be consistent from slide to slide; you don't want to use numbers on one slide and letters on the next.

customize bullets p. 49

- In the Text Inspector, you can also change the size of the bullet relative to the text, and change the bullet's vertical alignment.

add hyperlinks p. 51

- You can use graphic images as hyperlinks, not just text. So you can create buttons to link to any other slide, or anywhere else that Keynote can link to.

- To remove a hyperlink, select the link, open the Hyperlink Inspector, and clear the Enable as a hyperlink checkbox.

- As mentioned before, Keynote automatically turns URLs you type in the outline or slide into hyperlinks. You can turn this behavior off by choosing Keynote > Preferences, clicking the General section, then clearing the checkbox next to Automatically detect email and web addresses.

- Okay, I glossed over a few things above. Besides being able to create hyperlinks to a Web page or another slide in the same presentation, you can also create three other kinds of links: to open another Keynote file; create a new email message in your default email program; or exit the slideshow.

6. illustrate your presentation

The main look of your presentation will be supplied by the theme you select, but images add important spice to any presentation. Some information is better presented in a graphic form, and often you'll find that your audience will better grasp your message with graphical help. Your presentation can include many different kinds of information that isn't text, such as pictures, charts, diagrams, tables, clip art, sound effects, or video clips. Very few, if any, presentations include all of these elements, but you'll probably want to add at least some of them to every presentation.

This chapter is where you'll use the images and other media files that you gathered in Chapter 3. If you made a list of files and where they go, find and refer to it as you work through the chapter.

In this chapter, you'll learn how to add images and media clips to your presentation; use Keynote's drawing tools to add interest to your slides; import images from other applications; and add tables, diagrams, and charts to your presentation.

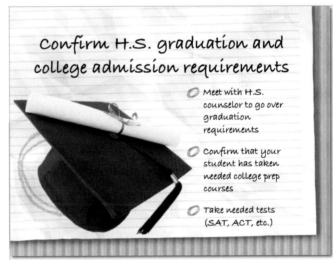

add iPhoto images

One of the new features in Keynote 2 is the Media palette, which integrates two of the programs from Apple's iLife suite—iTunes and iPhoto—thus making it easy to add music and photos to your presentation.

1 To add an image from your iPhoto library, display the slide where you want the image to go. You can place the image directly on the slide, or you can use a master slide with a placeholder or photo cutout ready to accept the image. If the master slide doesn't have a photo cutout, and you want such a layout, apply a master slide of this type using the instructions in Chapter 4. In the example opposite, I just put the image on the slide without a photo cutout.

2 If it isn't already visible, open the Media palette by clicking the Media button in the toolbar.

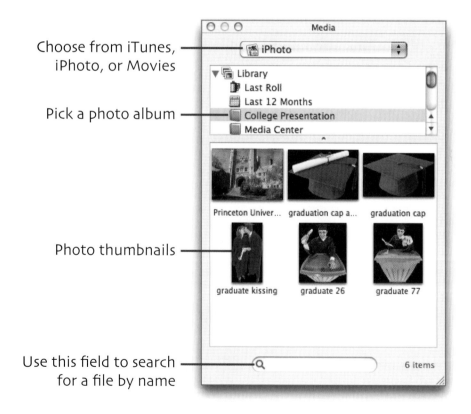

Choose from iTunes, iPhoto, or Movies

Pick a photo album

Photo thumbnails

Use this field to search for a file by name

illustrate your presentation

3 Use the pop-up menu at the top of the Media palette to view your iPhoto library.

4 Scroll through the list of photo albums, then select the one you want. The thumbnails for the images in that album appear.

5 Click and drag a thumbnail image from the Media palette onto your slide. The full-size photo appears on the slide.

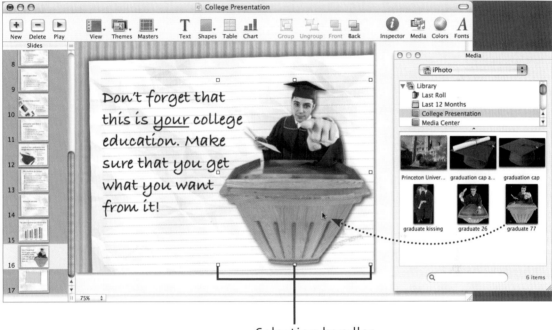

Selection handles

The image will appear with selection handles. Drag these handles to resize the image.

add images from disk

You can add pictures to your Keynote presentation that aren't in your iPhoto library by using files on your hard disk or on a CD and inserting them in the presentation.

1 Display the slide where you want the image to go. In this example, I'm using a master slide with a photo cutout.

2 The best way to work with photo cutouts is to make the image file visible in the Finder and drag and drop it from the Desktop onto the photo cutout on the slide. The image appears in the photo cutout, in a layer behind the slide background.

Photo cutout

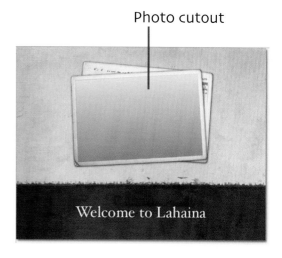

3 Note that the image's selection handles still appear on the slide. You can resize the image to make it fit better within the photo cutout by dragging the handles. Dragging any of the handles resizes the image proportionately. You can also click and drag the image within the cutout to reposition it in the cutout, or rotate the image to make it look better in the cutout.

If you prefer, you can place an image on a slide by choosing Insert > Choose, navigating to the image on your hard disk, and clicking Insert. The image will appear on your slide, but if you are using a master slide with a photo cutout, the image will not appear in the cutout. Instead, you'll have to send it to the back layer by first selecting the image and then clicking the Back button on the toolbar.

illustrate your presentation

use shapes

If you're the kind of person who can't draw a straight line, much less a circle or a diamond, then Keynote's shapes are for you. Keynote offers twelve ready-made shapes that can be easily placed onto your slides. These shapes include lines, arrows, rectangles, circles, and more.

To place a shape on your slide, choose from the Shapes pop-up menu in the toolbar. The corresponding shape appears on the slide. Here, I'm using the speech bubble shape for my slide.

Position the shape where you want it on the slide, and resize it if needed by dragging its handles.

style graphics

Keynote allows you to modify and enhance graphics in many different ways, such as by adding drop shadows; filling shapes with colors, images, or gradients; changing an image's opacity; adding a stroke, or border, around an image; rotating or flipping images; and grouping images. You've already seen examples of styling graphics; in the last section, I enhanced the look of the speech bubble by changing the fill color of the bubble to white; adding a one pixel black stroke around the edges of the bubble; and adding a drop shadow.

You'll use two of the Inspector panels to accomplish most of these common tasks, the Graphic Inspector and the Metrics Inspector.

Perhaps the most common special effect you'll add to an image is a drop shadow, which gives objects on your slides an appearance of depth. To add a drop shadow, select the image, then open the Graphic Inspector.

Shadow color well

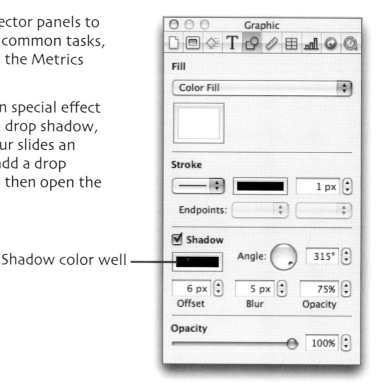

Click the Shadow checkbox, and the drop shadow will appear around the selected object. Use the controls in the Shadow section to adjust the angle of the shadow, its offset (how far away from the object the shadow extends), the thickness of the blur at the edge of the shadow, and the shadow's opacity. You can even click the color well to change the shadow's color; sometimes you can get a cool effect by using a colored shadow.

illustrate your presentation

To change the border of an object, use the Stroke section of the Graphic Inspector.

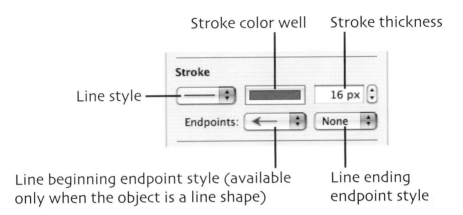

Stroke color well Stroke thickness

Line style

Line beginning endpoint style (available only when the object is a line shape)

Line ending endpoint style

Select the object, then choose a line style from the pop-up menu, change the color if desired, and adjust the stroke's thickness. If the object is one of Keynote's line shapes, you can also change the endpoints to arrow, circle, or box shapes.

You can fill shapes created in Keynote with solid colors, color gradients, or an image. A color fill replaces the interior of an object with a solid color, picked from the Colors palette. A gradient fill creates a smooth blend from one color that you set to a second color. An image fill replaces the interior of an object with any graphic image. A tinted image fill allows you to overlay a color tint on an image fill (for example, you could give a sepia tint to a photograph).

You'll use the Fill section of the Graphic Inspector to add fills. Select the object, then choose a fill type from the Fill pop-up menu. Depending on the kind of fill you choose, you may be able to make further adjustments; for example, if you choose an image fill, you can decide if you want to scale the image to fit into the object, stretch it to make it fill the shape, and more. Experiment with the settings to find the one you like.

style graphics (cont.)

By using the fill, stroke, shadow, and opacity controls, you can produce many interesting effects.

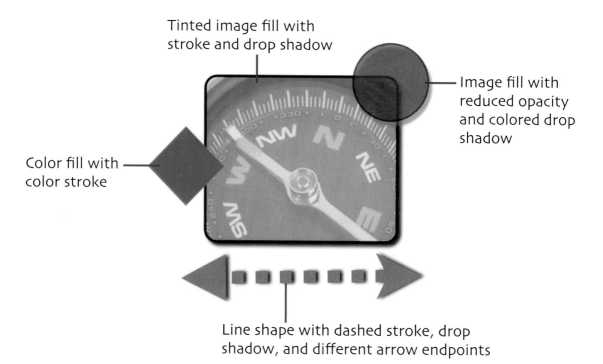

Tinted image fill with stroke and drop shadow

Image fill with reduced opacity and colored drop shadow

Color fill with color stroke

Line shape with dashed stroke, drop shadow, and different arrow endpoints

illustrate your presentation

rotate or flip objects

To rotate or flip an object, you'll use the Metrics Inspector. It's common to need to rotate images that you import, such as photos that you place into a photo cutout.

To flip an object around its horizontal or vertical axes, select the object and click one of the Flip buttons in the Metrics Inspector.

To rotate the image, select it on the slide and drag the angle wheel, or type a value into the Angle field.

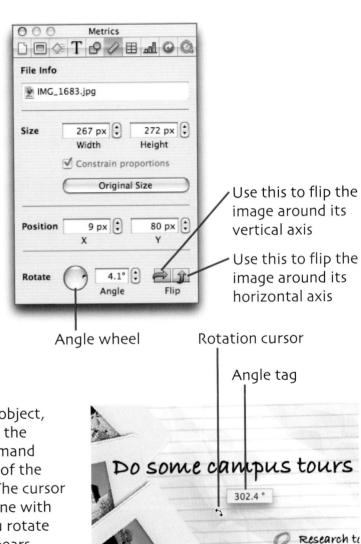

Use this to flip the image around its vertical axis

Use this to flip the image around its horizontal axis

Angle wheel

Rotation cursor

Angle tag

You can also free rotate an object, which is often faster. Select the object, hold down the Command key, and click and drag one of the object's selection handles. The cursor changes to a short curved line with arrows at both ends. As you rotate the object, an angle tag appears to show you the new angle for the object.

add music and sound

Usually, there's no quicker way to annoy your audience than by adding sounds to your slides. It's a big tip-off of novice presenters. But there are certainly valid reasons for using sounds in presentations. For example, a presentation about music might use brief clips, or anthropologists could include snippets of a language they are studying.

Keynote 2 adds the ability to use music or other sound files from your iTunes music library to your presentations. Remember that you can add almost any sound file to iTunes, so it can be easily available in Keynote or other programs such as iMovie.

Before you add sounds, you must decide if you want it as a soundtrack, which is music throughout an entire presentation, or as a sound on a single slide. Sound that plays on a single slide starts when the slide appears and stops when you move to the next slide.

1 Open the Media palette by clicking the Media button on the toolbar, then choose iTunes from the pop-up menu.

2 Scroll to the song or sound file you want, and select it in the list.

iTunes playlists

Song list

Click to preview the song or sound

Type here to find a song by name, artist, or album

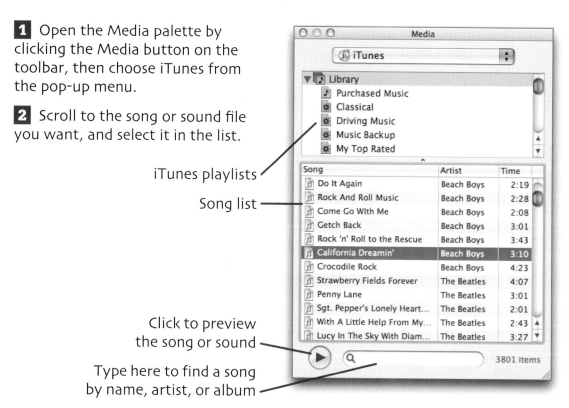

illustrate your presentation

3 If you want to add the sound as a soundtrack, open the Document Inspector, and drag the name of the sound into the sound well.

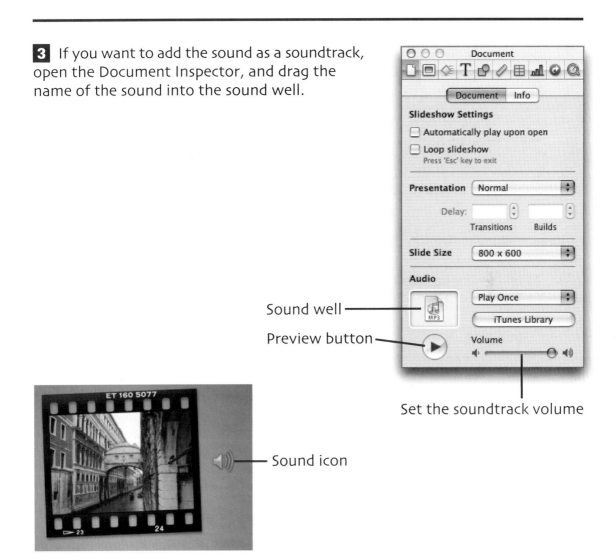

Sound well

Preview button

Set the soundtrack volume

Sound icon

4 If you want to put a sound on a single slide, select that slide in the Slide Navigator, then drag the sound from the Media palette onto the slide. A sound icon appears on the slide. Move it to where you want it; it will not appear when the presentation is running. To preview the sound, double-click the sound icon. During the presentation, the sound will start automatically.

use video clips

Video clips can be very effective in a presentation. You could include a video quote from your product manager, or show a brief tutorial. In the college presentation, I used a video clip to take audiences on a tour of one of the campuses we visited.

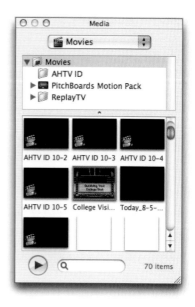

Movies you place in the Movies folder on your hard disk will appear in the Media palette, ready for you to use.

1 Open the Media palette by clicking the Media button on the toolbar, then choose Movies from the pop-up menu. Thumbnails of the movies in your Movies folder will appear.

2 Drag the thumbnail of the movie you want onto the slide. The movie appears on your slide. You might have to reposition and resize it.

If you want to play the movie to preview it, switch to the QuickTime Inspector and use its controls.

illustrate your presentation

add web views

When you're giving a presentation, it's not unusual to refer to a Web site where your audience can go for more information later. Keynote allows you to take a snapshot of a Web site, called a Web view, that is automatically updated with the current Web page when you run the slideshow (if your computer is connected to the Internet; if you're not connected, then the Web view shows the snapshot from the last time that you were connected).

The Web view is a hyperlink that you can click during the presentation to open the Web page in a browser.

To add a snapshot of a Web page, choose Insert > Web View. A snapshot of the default home page you've set in your browser appears, and the Inspector window automatically changes to the Hyperlink Inspector.

Because the default home page probably isn't what you want in your presentation, you need to change the target of the Web view in the Hyperlink Inspector. Type the address of the Web page you want in the URL field, then press Return. If your computer is connected to the Internet, the Web view on the slide changes to show the site you just entered.

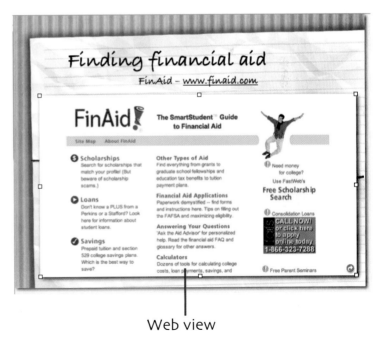

Web view

add charts

Many slide presentations include a set of numbers of some kind—for example, projected fundraising for next year, or a look back at last year's budget versus actual numbers. It's difficult for an audience to understand long columns of numbers, especially in the short time they would be on the screen during your presentation. A chart offers a much better way to let people quickly grasp the relationship between numbers and helps them spot trends.

To add a chart to one of your slides, start by first creating a new slide, and apply an appropriate master slide (usually the Blank or Title – Top master slide). Then click the Chart button on the toolbar, or choose Insert > Chart.

Three things happen: a chart appears on the slide, the Inspector changes to the Chart Inspector, and a new window, called the Chart Data Editor, appears.

By default, the Chart Data Editor contains two rows and four columns of sample data, so that you can get an idea of what the chart will look like. Select and change the sample data in the Chart Data Editor one cell at a time, entering your own data. As you change data in the Chart Data Editor, the chart automatically updates.

Chart legend

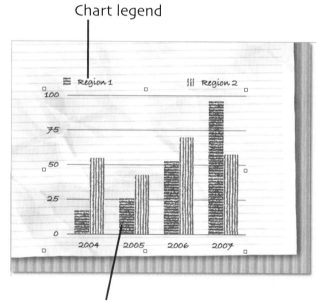

New chart using sample data

To change the labels in the chart legend, double-click them in the Chart Data Editor, and when they highlight, type the new legend.

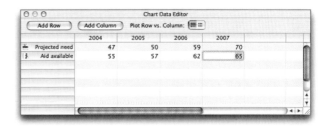

Use the Chart Inspector to make any other changes you need in the chart, such as changing the chart type, the chart layout, and so on. Keynote has eight built-in chart types: Column, Stacked Column, Bar, Stacked Bar, Line, Area, Stacked Area, and Pie.

Chart Type pop-up menu

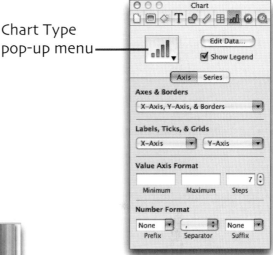

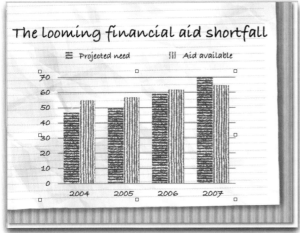

If you want to change chart colors, add strokes to bars, add shadows, or change the chart's opacity, select a bar in the chart and use the Graphic Inspector. If needed, add a text box to act as a title for your chart.

add tables

Tables are a great way to show relationships between groups of data, and to get a lot of information into your presentation in an easy to understand fashion. Tables can contain words, numbers, or both.

On the toolbar, click the Table button. The table grid appears, and the Inspector switches to the Table Inspector.

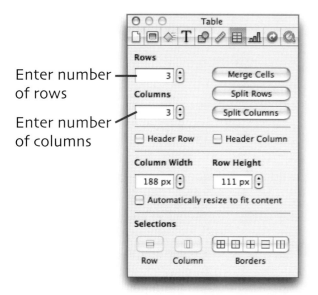

Enter number of rows

Enter number of columns

If you want, click on a horizontal or vertical line inside the table, and the cursor turns into a double-headed arrow. Then click and drag to resize the rows or columns.

Click inside the first cell of the table to get an insertion point, then enter your data into the cells. You can press the Tab key to move between cells without using the mouse. When you're finished adding data to the table, click on the slide background to deselect the table.

You can use the Table Inspector to merge and split rows or columns, and the Format > Table submenu gives you many more options to format the table, such as adding rows and columns, and the ability to distribute selected rows or columns evenly, which saves you a lot of time fiddling with row heights and column widths.

Eligibility requirements

Subject	Cal State University	University of California
History	2 years (plus another year from list)	2 years (plus another course from list)
English	4 years	
Mathematics	3 years (4 recommended)	
Lab Science	2 years (1 yr physical, 1 yr bio)	2 years (inc. 2 of 3: biology, chemistry, or physics)
Language	2 years	3 years recommended
Arts	1 year	
College Prep Elective	1 year	

illustrate your presentation

extra bits

add iPhoto images p. 58

- If you select Library in the Media palette's scrolling list, you can browse through all of the images in your iPhoto library.

- Images with transparent masks, such as a photo-object from some clip art collections, may appear in iPhoto as if they have a black background. Don't worry; when you drag them from the Media palette into Keynote, the image will appear with its correct transparency.

add images from disk p. 60

- You can also add an image to a slide by dragging and dropping it from the Desktop on to your slide. Sometimes this is faster than navigating through the Open dialog.

- To delete an imported graphic or Keynote shape, select it, and press Delete.

use shapes p. 61

- Once you place a shape, you cannot change it to a different kind of shape. For example, you can't convert a rectangle into a circle.

- You can layer text and graphics, so if you want to, for example, put text inside a callout shape, you would insert a text box over the callout shape.

- As you may have figured out, Keynote's selection of shapes and drawing abilities are quite limited. There's a darned good drawing program that works great with Keynote, and it may already be on your Mac. It's called OmniGraffle, from Omni Development (www.omnigroup. com). OmniGraffle is great for creating diagrams, flowcharts, and shapes that Keynote can't make, and it's an excellent tool for drawing custom bullets.

  Graphics created in OmniGraffle can be exported as PDF. They retain their transparency, so they scale well and play well with other slide elements. You can draw shapes in OmniGraffle, fill them with images, and then export them to Keynote.

  The reason you may already have OmniGraffle is that Apple has bundled it with their professional-level machines (Power Mac G4, PowerMac G5, and PowerBooks). Check in your Applications folder. If you don't have the program, it's only $70, with a Professional version that includes more features for $120.

extra bits

- If you need to precisely line up objects, you'll find alignment and distribution commands in the Arrange menu.

- You can easily add an organizational chart, if you have a copy of Microsoft Office. In Word, Excel, or PowerPoint, choose Insert > Object, then from the resulting Object dialog, choose Microsoft Organization Chart and click OK. A separate program, also called Microsoft Organization Chart, opens and lets you create and adjust the org chart. When you're done, close the program, and the new org chart is automatically pasted into your Office document. From there you can copy and paste it into your Keynote presentation file.

style graphics p. 62

- If you have more than one object with drop shadows on a slide, it usually looks better to give all the objects the same shadow values.

- You can copy and paste shadow settings from one object to another by selecting the first object, choosing Format > Copy Style, selecting the second object, and choosing Format >

Paste Style. This also copies the stroke, fill, and opacity settings.

- Once you have objects precisely where you want them on the Slide Canvas, it's annoying to accidentally select and move them when you're trying to move another object. Prevent that problem by choosing Arrange > Lock and locking the object, which makes the object immovable. You can still select a locked object, but the only thing that you can do to it is unlock it; you can't move it or change any of its properties until it is unlocked by choosing Arrange > Unlock. When an object is locked, each of its selection handles turn from a small square into an x.

illustrate your presentation

- Keynote can't crop imported graphics, but it can mask them. A mask gives you the effect of cropping without actually modifying the image. To mask an image, select the image and choose Format > Mask. A mask overlay, looking like a selection rectangle, appears over the image. Drag the mask's selection handles to adjust the area of the image you want to show. Press Return; the image is masked and areas of the image outside the mask won't appear.

- If you have several graphic objects on a slide, you might find it easier to work with them as a group. You can move the group on the slide, or copy and paste it between slides, which is much easier than selecting individual objects. Grouping objects also preserves their positions relative to one another. To group objects, select them and choose Group from the toolbar, or choose Arrange > Group. You'll now see one set of selection handles for the group.

add music and sound p. 66

- Keynote supports any audio type that QuickTime does, including AAC, AIFF, AU, MIDI, MOV, MP3, SFIL, and WAV.

- To delete a soundtrack, drag the sound icon out of the sound well in the Document Inspector and release the mouse button. The icon will disappear in a puff of animated smoke.

- Depending on your presentation setting, it can be effective to attach a music file to the beginning and end slides of your presentation, which helps introduce and end the show.

- You can drag iTunes playlists from the Media palette into the Document Inspector or onto a slide, instead of a single song.

use video clips p. 68

- Keynote supports any video type that QuickTime does, including AVI, DV, Flash (SWF), MPEG, and MOV.

extra bits

add web views p. 69

- A Web view often looks better on your slide if you add a drop shadow to it with the Graphic Inspector.

- If you have a Web view in your presentation, and you know that you will be presenting at a location that doesn't have Internet access, use the Update Now button on the Hyperlink Inspector while you still have a connection, just before you leave for your presentation.

add charts p. 70

- Keynote's charting abilities are decent, but they are hardly complete. For example, Keynote doesn't provide 3-D charts, and it lacks many chart types found in other charting programs. Keynote also lacks the ability to create combination charts, which contain more than one chart type. If you need more charting power than Keynote can provide, you'll need to turn to other applications that can create charts, such as Microsoft Excel or Chartsmith, from Blacksmith (www.blacksmith.com), a standalone charting application for Mac OS X. Either application provides many more chart types for your charting excitement.

- Besides entering chart data directly in Keynote's Chart Data Editor, you can also copy and paste spreadsheet data from Microsoft Excel or AppleWorks into the Chart Data Editor.

- If you're more comfortable working with charts in Microsoft Excel, you can create a chart in Excel, copy it, then paste it into a Keynote slide. Of course, it will then be treated as a graphic, and you won't be able to change the data in Keynote.

- You'll see how to animate charts in Chapter 7.

add tables p. 72

- Table cells can contain graphics, as well as text.

- You can copy the contents of one table cell into another by Option-dragging it. If you select multiple cells (like a row or a column) before you Option-drag, the contents of all the cells will be copied into the destination cells.

- You'll see how to animate tables in Chapter 7.

illustrate your presentation

7. make it move

Your presentation is nearly complete. You've written the content, chosen a theme, set a master slide for each slide, and added images and media files. The last major task before you get ready to give the presentation is to give the presentation some movement, by adding slide transitions and slide builds.

Slide transitions are the animated effects the audience sees when you switch from one slide to the next in the presentation. Keynote provides many different transition effects. Object builds are animations that occur within a slide. For example, you can have each bullet point fade onto the screen as you get to it. Or you can have an image, graph, or diagram glide onto the screen.

In this chapter, you'll learn how to rearrange the order of your slides in the Slide Navigator and then set slide transitions and object build effects.

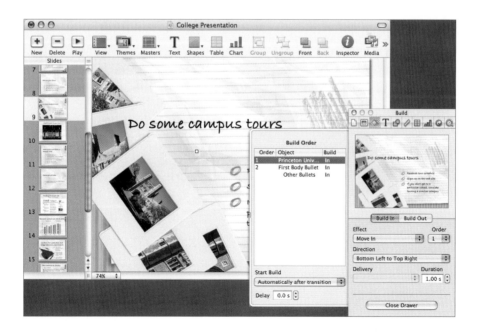

rearrange slides

As you've been developing your presentation, you've seen how the topic of one slide flows into the next, and perhaps that flow is perfect for your show. But maybe the presentation would be a bit better, a touch tighter, if you moved that slide there, and moved that other slide over here. Keynote's Slide Navigator allows you to drag one or more slides to other places in the presentation. The Slide Navigator is also a convenient way to apply slide transitions to multiple slides in one operation (you'll see how to do that in the next section).

If you're not already in Slide Navigator view, choose View > Navigator. In Slide Navigator view, you see thumbnail views of the slides; the currently selected slide has a yellow border around it and a lighter background.

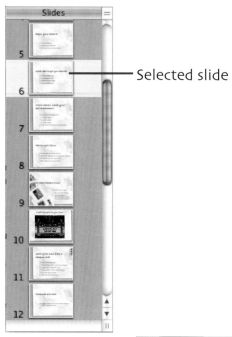

Selected slide

To move a slide, click on the slide you want to move, then drag it to the new location. As you drag, a blue indicator line with a triangle will show you where the slide will go when you release the mouse button.

Original slide position

New slide position when mouse button is released

make it move

set slide transitions

Transitions between slides can enhance your presentation's message and add visual interest to your show. You can add transitions to one or more slides at one time in the Slide Navigator. Keynote includes many transition effects to choose from, ranging from subtle to the polar opposite of subtle. When choosing transitions, as with any animation in Keynote, you should live by the principle "less is more," because the flashier they are, the more quickly your audience will become tired of them.

You use the Slide Inspector to set slide transitions.

1 If it isn't already open, click the Inspector button on the toolbar to open the Inspector, then click the Slide Inspector button.

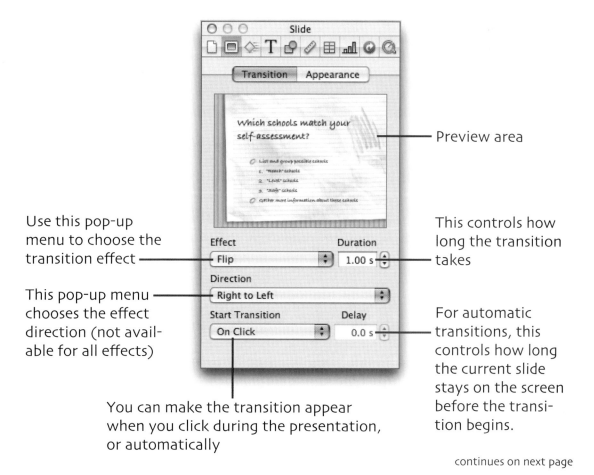

Preview area

Use this pop-up menu to choose the transition effect

This controls how long the transition takes

This pop-up menu chooses the effect direction (not available for all effects)

For automatic transitions, this controls how long the current slide stays on the screen before the transition begins.

You can make the transition appear when you click during the presentation, or automatically

continues on next page

make it move   **79**

set slide transitions (cont.)

2 In the Slide Navigator, select the slides to which you want to apply the transitions. To select multiple slides, click on the first slide, hold down the Shift key, and click the last slide. Those slides and all slides in between are selected.

3 Choose a transition effect from the Effect pop-up menu. You'll see the effect in the preview area of the Inspector. You can try out different transition effects here, and decide on the one you like.

4 Choose the speed of the transition by selecting it in the Duration field. Often, you can leave it set to the default value of 1 second.

5 Many transitions can be set to move in a particular direction. For example, the Wipe effect can move from left to right, right to left, top to bottom, or bottom to top. If the effect you chose has a movement option, choose it from the Direction pop-up menu.

None
3D Effects
Cube
✓ Flip
Mosaic Flip Large
Mosaic Flip Small
Page Flip
2D Effects
Burn
Dissolve
Drop
Droplet
Fade Through Black
Falling Tiles
Flash
Grid
Iris
Motion Dissolve
Move In
Pivot
Push
Radial
Reveal
Scale
Twirl
Wipe

6 In the Start Transition pop-up menu, you have two choices. On Click requires you to click the mouse or press one of the arrow keys on the keyboard during the presentation to trigger the transition. This is probably the setting you'll use the most. Automatically will play the transition to the next slide as soon as any object builds on the slide are complete and the amount of time you set in the Delay field elapses.

You know that a slide has a transition applied to it because a blue triangle appears in the slide's thumbnail in the Slide Navigator.

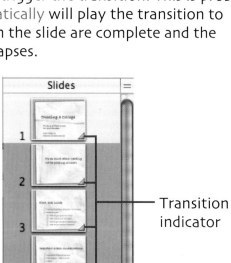

Transition indicator

make it move

add object builds

The generic name for an animation that occurs on a single slide is an object build. When you create a build, you can set the way the object "builds in" (appears on the slide) and "builds out" (leaves the slide). You control the build process with the Build Inspector. On that Inspector, the Build In and Build Out tabs set the build options.

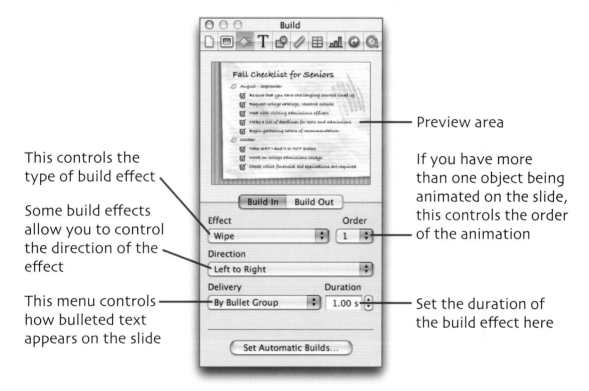

This controls the type of build effect

Some build effects allow you to control the direction of the effect

This menu controls how bulleted text appears on the slide

Preview area

If you have more than one object being animated on the slide, this controls the order of the animation

Set the duration of the build effect here

Probably the most common build you will apply is with bulleted text; use it to make each bullet and its associated text appear when you click the mouse button during the presentation. These text builds can be set up with a number of options so that you can control how the text appears on the slide.

1 If it isn't already open, click the Inspector button on the toolbar to open the Inspector, then click the Build Inspector button.

2 Begin setting the text build by switching to a slide with bulleted text, and then select the bulleted text box.

continues on next page

make it move

add object builds (cont.)

3 By default, the Build In tab is selected. If you want to create a Build Out, click that tab. Otherwise, continue on the Build In tab.

4 From the Effect pop-up menu, choose the type of animation you want. Whenever you make a change in the Build Inspector, you'll see a thumbnail preview of the build in the Inspector's preview area.

5 From the Direction pop-up menu, choose the direction from which you want bulleted text to move onto the slide.

6 From the Delivery pop-up menu, choose one of the following:

All at Once builds the entire contents of the bulleted text box onto or off of the slide.

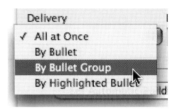

By Bullet builds each bullet point onto or off of the slide one bullet point at a time. Second-level bullets animate separately.

By Bullet Group also builds each bullet point onto or off of the slide, but second-level bullets animate with their parents.

By Highlighted Bullet builds each bullet point on the slide and when you go to the next bullet point, the one you just left dims. The current bullet point always looks most prominent.

Depending on the object you have selected, the context-sensitive Delivery menu may contain different items.

7 If you want to create a Build Out, click the Build Out tab, then repeat steps 3 through 5.

Builds for other objects, such as graphics or shapes, work much the same way (except, of course, you won't have the bullet-related options in the Delivery menu).

You can tell that a slide has object builds in the Slide Navigator; the slide has three small dots in its upper-right corner.

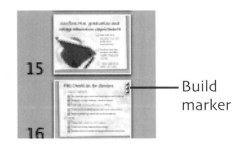

Build marker

set automatic builds

Keynote 2 added the ability to make object builds happen automatically and greatly improved the control you have over the way objects appear on slides. You'll find the controls for this new feature in the Automatic Build drawer in the Build Inspector. To open this drawer, click the Set Automatic Builds button at the bottom of the Build Inspector. The drawer slides out of the Inspector.

Automatic Build drawer

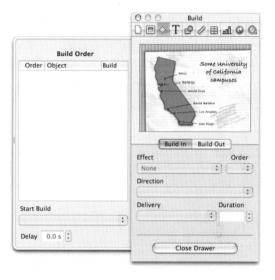

In this example, there are three objects on the slide.

The slide title

This graphic image of California was imported from OmniGraffle.

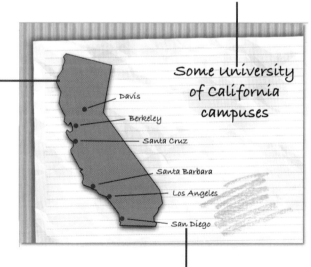

The dots, lines, and campus names were created in Keynote, positioned, then grouped so they act like a single object.

continues on next page

make it move

set automatic builds (cont.)

We're just going to animate the graphic and the campus name group, because it would look tacky to also animate the slide title. Select the California shape. In the Build Inspector, the Effect pop-up menu becomes active. Choose the Scale effect, which will make the image of the state zoom into view, then choose from the Direction pop-up menu and set the Duration of the build. The build plays in the preview area and appears in the Automatic Build drawer.

We want the build to occur as soon as the slide appears. Choose Automatically after transition from the Start Build menu. If we want a pause before the build begins, enter the amount of time in the Delay field.

make it move

Select the campus name group and set a Wipe effect, with the direction Top to Bottom. This makes the names appear from north to south along the length of the state, a nice effect. The second build appears in the Automatic Build drawer. We don't want to click to make it appear, so choose Automatically after build 1 from the Start Build menu. We could have chosen Automatically with build 1; that would make the campus name group appear at the same time the state image was zooming in, but it would look goofy.

Because there's no substitute for looking at the real thing, save the presentation, then click Play on the toolbar to see how the build looks with the full-size slide. In this case, I wasn't happy with the timing of the campus name group animation (too slow), so I selected the number 2 build in the Automatic Build drawer and reduced the Duration in the Build Inspector.

animate charts

Chart builds rank just behind bulleted text builds in usefulness. You can get some dramatic effects when you make the parts of a chart appear sequentially on the screen.

To animate a chart, switch to a slide with the chart you want to animate and display the Build Inspector. On the slide, select the chart.

The slide appears in the preview area of the Inspector. Choose Wipe from the Effect pop-up menu and the controls change to work with charts.

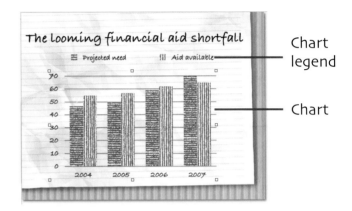

Chart legend

Chart

Because the chart is a column chart, choose Bottom to Top from the Direction menu, so the chart columns appear to "grow up" from the bottom. The Delivery menu for charts gives you a variety of nice effects that make different parts of the chart appear in different orders. Try them and see which one you like.

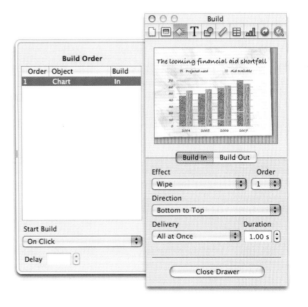

make it move

If you choose anything in the Delivery menu other than All at Once, you'll see a sub-build in the Automatic Build drawer. The sub-build controls the elements of the main build. As with any other build, you can set this sub-build in the Start Build pop-up menu to trigger automatically or with a click.

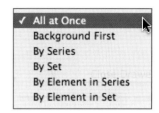

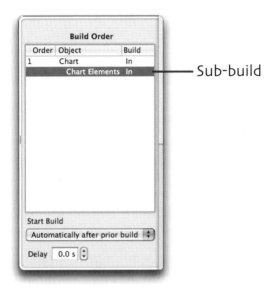 ——— Sub-build

The chart legend is treated as separate from the rest of the chart. You can apply a different build setting to it, or if you want it to move with the rest of the chart, select the chart and the legend, and group them by clicking the Group button in the toolbar before you apply any build styles. In this case, apply a separate build effect to the chart legend (a Wipe from Top to Bottom), and set it to appear Automatically with build 1. ———

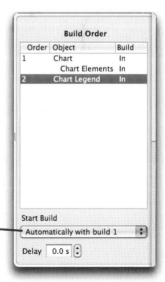

add table builds

You can animate Keynote tables so that the parts of the table appear on the screen in sequence. This adds some visual flair to the table and can even add a touch of drama. It's especially effective to have the contents of a table build in to your slide. With tables, you can control the direction and delivery options of your builds.

In this example of building a table, switch to a slide with the table you want to animate, then display the Build Inspector. On the slide, select the table.

From the Effect pop-up menu, choose the build style you want, then pick from the Direction pop-up menu. You have several different Delivery options for tables.

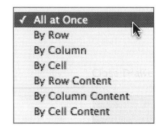

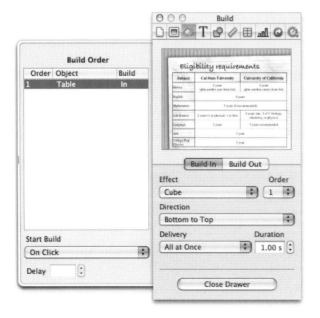

Set the rest of the options as you would other object builds. When you're done setting the build, you will have at least one build in the Automatic Build window. Depending on your choice from the Delivery menu, you may have one or more sub-builds listed, too.

make it move

extra bits

rearrange slides p. 78

- If you want to move a group of slides all together, in Slide Navigator view, click the first slide, hold down the Shift key, and click the last slide. Those two slides and all slides in between will be selected, and you can drag and drop them as a group.

- The Slide Navigator also lets you group slides by indenting related slides. Indenting slides doesn't change the final presentation. It's a tool that helps you organize large sets of slides. Once you have grouped slides together, you can show or hide groups to make it easier for you to work with and organize the presentation.

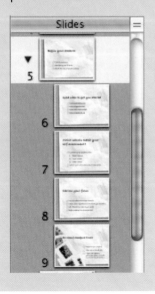

To group slides, select one or more slides that you want to indent under another slide, then press Tab. The slide(s) are indented, and a disclosure triangle appears next to the slide above the indented slide. You can click this triangle to hide or show the indented slides in the Slide Navigator. To ungroup slides, select them and press Shift-Tab.

- You can skip slides that you don't want to show in your presentation. For example, you might want to give the same basic presentation to two different audiences, but omit some slides for a particular audience. Rather than make two different presentations, just set some slides to be skipped before you go to talk to the second group. Select the slide or slides you want to skip, then choose Slide > Skip Slide. The slide thumbnail in the Slide Navigator will collapse to a line.

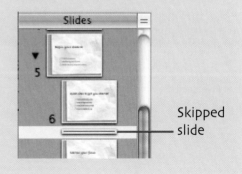

Skipped slide

extra bits

The slide will not appear when you play the presentation. To show the slide again, select the slide and choose Slide > Don't Skip Slide.

- If you indent and group slides, skipping the top slide in the group skips all of the slides in the group when you play the presentation.

set slide transitions p. 79

- You'll often find that the preview of the transition in the Slide Inspector isn't really sufficient to tell if the transition feels right for your presentation. I suggest that you apply a transition to two or three slides, select the first one, then click Play in the toolbar to preview the transition at full size. Press the Escape key to leave the slideshow, and then if necessary, you can pick another transition effect.

- You can use slide transitions to communicate different types of information or to denote sections in your presentation. For example, you can use a transition to signify that you're moving to an entirely different topic in your presentation. Let's say that you have a presentation with three distinct sections. You can use no transitions between the slides in each section, and use transitions only between slides at the end of one section and the beginning of the next. Or use one sort of transition for most slides, and use a very different one between sections.

- When it comes to slide transitions, restraint really should be the order of the day. Chances are you've seen presentations where presenters used way too many transitions and animated effects. Did you like them? No? That's what I thought.

Too-busy slide transitions and animations of objects on the slide can easily distract the audience from the content of your presentation. Make sure not to overdo them, or you might find your audience slipping out of the room before your talk is over—which is not the sign of a successful presentation. Too much swooping and spinning can even make some audience members nauseous!

make it move

add object builds p. 81

- For text boxes (not bulleted text boxes), there is another option in the Delivery menu. By Paragraph moves text in text boxes one paragraph at a time.
- Build or delay durations can be from one-tenth of one second to 60 seconds in length.

set automatic builds p. 83

- If you want to change the order of builds, click and drag the build you want to change in the Automatic Builds drawer.
- To make more than two objects appear at the same time, group them before you apply the build effect.
- If you group or ungroup an object that has a build effect applied to it, Keynote removes the build effect.
- You can use sound files in builds; this is useful, for example, if you want a sound to begin after another object appears.

animate charts p. 86

- You can create more interesting chart builds by using the Graphic Inspector to replace the image fills for the chart elements with shapes. For a build like this, the Wipe build style, with the Direction set to Bottom to Top and Delivery set to By Set, is especially effective.

add table builds p. 88

- Using the Wipe build style is especially nice for tables; the wipe has a soft edge that looks quite attractive.

make it move

8. prepare to present

Now that you've finished putting together your presentation, there are some things you can do to make it better before you "step on stage." The easiest way to improve your talk is familiar to anyone who has done any kind of performance: rehearse it before you get in front of your audience. You can also send your presentation to co-workers for their comments; it's amazing how often other people will suggest a great point that you missed.

To help you give the presentation, you can create and print speaker notes, and to help the audience, you can print handouts containing your slides. In this chapter, you'll see how a little final preparation can help make your presentation a smashing success.

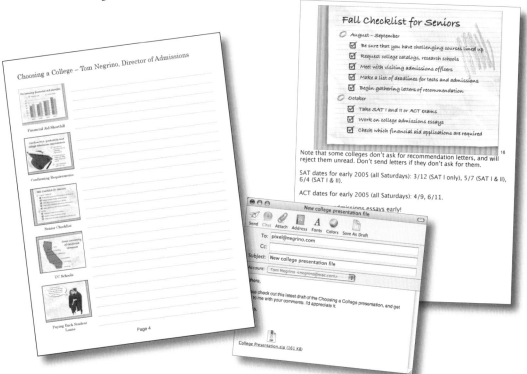

get colleague review

One easy way to improve your presentation is to show it to other people for their comments. You'll often gain valuable insights into your presentation by getting this feedback. I've had some co-workers suggest areas that I should have mentioned, and others give me some great images that I incorporated into my show. If possible, allow people to watch you rehearse, then solicit their constructive criticism. Believe me, your final presentation will be better for it.

There are two ways to share your presentation with a co-worker. If you know that the recipient has Keynote 2, you can simply email them your presentation file. If they don't have Keynote, I suggest that you export the presentation as a PDF file, which can be read by any Mac OS X user (with the included Preview application or with the free downloadable Adobe Reader). If your recipient isn't a Mac user, Adobe Reader is available for Windows, Linux, and most other common computer platforms.

To send your presentation file to colleagues as an email attachment, you'll have to first make an archive. The reason for that is because a Keynote presentation file is actually a package, which is a special folder that Mac OS X shows as an icon, but which really contains multiple files. The problem is that email programs don't work well with package files. By using Mac OS X's built-in ability to turn the presentation file into an archive, you'll ensure that the file gets through in good shape.

To turn a presentation file into an archive, first locate the file in the Finder.

Click once on the Keynote file to select it, then choose File > Create Archive of [name of the file]. The Finder will create the archive file, which will have the name of the presentation file plus the suffix .zip.

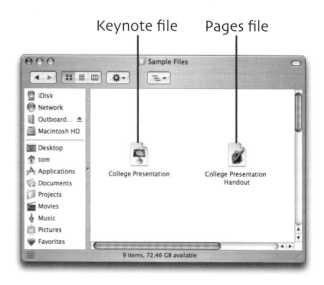

Keynote file   Pages file

prepare to present

Now open your email program and create a new message (the procedure for this will differ slightly, depending on the program you use). Address the email, enter a note for your recipient, include the archive file as an attachment, and send the message on its way.

On the other end, your recipient will have to expand the archive file before it can be read by Keynote. All they need to do is save the attached file from their incoming email onto their hard disk, then double-click the file. Mac OS X will turn it back into a Keynote file.

Archive file

College Presentation.zip

College Presentation

get colleague review (cont.)

If your recipient doesn't have Keynote, you can turn the presentation into a PDF file. The drawback is that your colleague won't be able to see any animations or transitions, so they can't get a full understanding of your show. But at least they can review the content.

To turn your presentation into a PDF, choose File > Export. The Export dialog appears. Click the PDF radio button.

Click Next. In the resulting Save dialog, decide where you want to save the file, give the PDF file a name, and click Export. The file is saved on your hard disk.

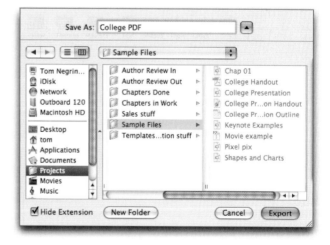

If you want, you can open the file in a PDF application to check it, such as in Adobe Reader, shown here. Otherwise, you can attach the PDF file to an email message and send it off. You don't need to archive the PDF file.

rehearse your show

Rehearsals are key to any production, whether it is a Broadway play, a concert, or your slideshow. When you rehearse your presentation, you get a better feel for what you want to say to accompany the slides, and it helps you make sure that you stay within your allotted time. Being able to do the whole presentation at your own pace is infinitely preferable to trying to stretch if you run short, or worse, getting the hook if you run too long. Unless you have a lot of experience presenting, rehearsal is the best way to find out how long your presentation really is.

If you feel silly rehearsing a presentation out loud to an empty room, join the club; we all do. But try it anyway. You'll be sure to improve your presentation. In fact, I suggest that you consider rehearsing at least once in front of a mirror, or set up a video camera and record your rehearsal. It may feel a tad excruciating the first time, but you'll get a much better idea of your facial expressions and mannerisms, and it will help you get your timing right, too.

To do a rehearsal, you'll need two things: Keynote and a countdown timer (because you usually know how much time you're allotted for your talk). Keynote, as it happens, comes with a countdown timer, but it can only be used when you're in the Presenter Display, so it's not very useful for rehearsals unless you have an external monitor or projector available for the rehearsal. You'll learn more about the Presenter Display in Chapter 9.

In the meantime, if all you need is a simple countdown timer, let me suggest a freeware alternative called Tea Timer, which you can download from www.herwig-henseler.de/software/teatimer.html. Now, this countdown timer is literally meant to tell you when your tea has finished steeping, but it works great for any of your countdown needs. Just download it and put it in your Applications folder. When you run it, you get a simple window.

Put the amount of time you have for your presentation in the Tea Timer window, and click OK. Switch to Keynote and click Play on the toolbar. Rehearse your presentation. While you are doing so, Tea Timer is counting down in the background. You won't see Tea Timer's countdown window while the presentation is onscreen, but you will hear its alarm when the timer reaches zero (the sound of Big Ben's chimes). If you still have part of your presentation left, you'll know that you need to speed up parts of your talk, or even that you'll need to trim it to fit in the allotted time.

create speaker notes

Speaker Notes are printed notes that you'll use to help keep you on track while you're giving the presentation. As you saw way back in Chapter 1, Keynote has a Notes area where you can type in your notes for each slide.

These notes don't appear on the presentation screen, but if you're using a laptop to present with an external projector or monitor, the notes will appear on the laptop screen, so you can see them, but your audience can't.

Speaker Notes

If you prefer, you can also print speaker Notes (let's say that you won't be operating the computer yourself) so that you can refer to notes without being tethered to your computer. When Keynote prints speaker Notes, they appear one slide to a page, with your notes underneath.

To print the speaker Notes, choose File > Print. From the Copies & Pages pop-up menu, choose Keynote.

Choose Keynote from this pop-up menu

In the Keynote section of the Print dialog, click Slides With Notes, then click Print.

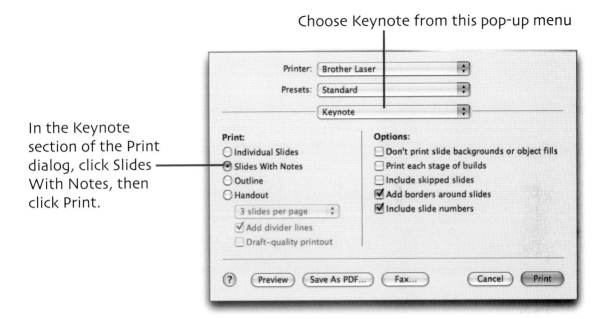

print slides & handouts

You can print slides and handouts for your use (or for the audience) in color (with a color printer, of course), grayscale, or black and white. When you print slides, just the slide appears on the page, filling the page, in landscape format (meaning the slide is rotated so that the wide side of the slide is aligned with the length of the printed page).

For handouts, Keynote gives you a choice of 2, 3, 4, 5, or 6 slides per printed page, shrinking the slides to fit. If you want your audience to be able to take notes easily, I suggest that you use the 4 slides per page option; the slides are a good size for easy legibility.

To print slides, choose File > Print. In the Print dialog, choose Keynote from the Copies & Pages pop-up menu. In the Keynote section of the Print dialog, choose Individual Slides, then click Print to print the slides.

To print handouts, choose File > Print. In the Print dialog, choose Keynote from the Copies & Pages pop-up menu. In the Keynote section of the Print dialog, choose Handout, then pick the number of slides per page from the pop-up menu. I suggest that you also turn on the Add divider lines, Add borders around slides and Include slide numbers options in the Print dialog.

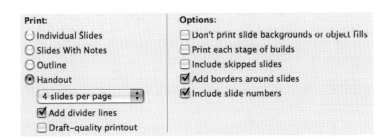

The handouts that Keynote gives you are not great, to be frank. You would have thought that Apple would have found a way to leverage the capabilities of Pages, the other program in the iWork suite, to produce better-looking handouts. One person has stepped in to offer a free Keynote handout template made in Pages, however. You'll find it on KeynoteUser.com, at

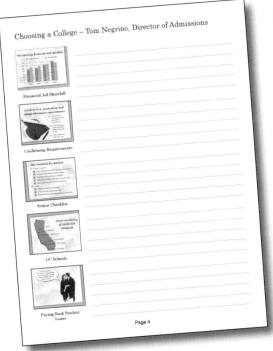

www.keynoteuser.com/downloads/other.html. This handout allows you to put five slides on a page, includes a place for the presentation's title, and provides lines next to the slides for audience notes. You'll need to export your slides from Keynote as separate images (choose File > Export, then choose Images). You'll then need to drag the images into the Pages template one by one and scale them to fit the template. It's a bit of work, but you'll get a much nicer result.

extra bits

get colleague review p. 94

- The archive file format is ZIP, which is a standard archive format that can be read and decompressed by virtually all kinds of computers. One other benefit of turning your Keynote files into archives for email is that archive files are also compressed, meaning that they take up less disk space. The archiving process uses a mathematical algorithm that packs the file more tightly. This compression is often significant; for example, the presentation file for this book's project is about 750K, and when archived, is only 370K. That means the archived files transmit via email in less time, too.

- You don't need to compress a PDF file before sending it because PDF files are already compressed; compression is built into the PDF format.

- If you don't already have it, you can get the free Adobe Reader so you can view PDF files by pointing your browser to www.adobe.com/reader/. You might be wondering why you want the Adobe Reader, since Preview is already included with Mac OS X and does a good job of reading PDFs. It's because there are some PDF files

with advanced PDF features that work better in Reader than in Preview. Another reason is that Reader comes with a plug-in for the Safari Web browser that allows you to conveniently view PDF files on the Web right in the browser, instead of having to download them and open them in Preview.

- Another possibility for colleague review is to export your Keynote presentation as a PowerPoint file, if your recipient has Microsoft Office. This is an especially attractive prospect if your colleague is on Windows. The drawback to PowerPoint export is that Keynote has some transitions and effects that don't translate exactly to PowerPoint. But for many presentations, it works well enough. To export as a PowerPoint file, choose File > Export, then choose PowerPoint in the Export dialog. Click Export and save the file on your hard disk. You won't have to make an archive of the PowerPoint file before you send it via email, unless you want to compress it to reduce the file size.

- You can also export the Keynote file as a QuickTime movie or Flash file. You'll learn more about those options in Chapter 10.

rehearse your show p. 98

- When you're rehearsing timings, it's a good idea to speak your narration just as you would during the presentation. Stand up or sit up straight, breathe normally, and speak clearly without rushing.

print slides & handouts p. 102

- It's almost always a good idea to preview the slides on screen before you print them. In the Print dialog, click the Preview button to open the print job in the Preview application.

- You can use the Pages controls in the Print dialog to print all slides, or a range of slides, when printing either slides or handouts.

- You have the option of printing slides with or without builds. If you print with builds, you will get as many slides printed as you have slide effects. For example, let's say you have a slide with a title and three bullet points. The bullet points wipe onto the screen one by one. Printing the slide with builds means that you'll get four pages, one for the slide with just the title, and then one more page for each bullet point. Most of the time, you'll want to print slides without animations.

- If your slides have dark backgrounds, they won't print very legibly on black and white printers. In that case, check Don't print slide backgrounds or object fills in the Keynote section of the Print dialog. The backgrounds won't print, and white text will reverse to black so that it will be visible.

- You can also print the presentation outline. Just click Outline in the Keynote section of the Print dialog.

9. deliver your presentation

Finally, you're ready to give your presentation. You've arrived at the room where you'll give the talk, and perhaps the audience is beginning to arrive. You need to connect your laptop computer to the projector, set up your computer so that it recognizes the two displays (the laptop screen and the projector), and run the show.

If you don't have a laptop computer, and you know that the presentation venue will have a computer with Keynote 2 installed and a projector waiting for you, you can burn your presentation to a CD and just bring that.

During the presentation, you can use Keynote's Presenter Display, which allows you to control your show and to display your speaker Notes as you present, using an interface that only you see.

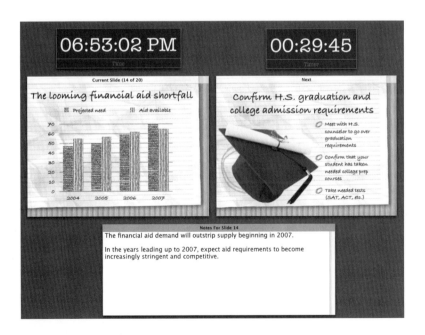

set up the projector

You'll typically want to deliver a presentation with a laptop computer connected to a projector or large monitor. Your computer must support multiple monitors (most Apple laptops do; some older iBooks did not have a video-out port). You'll view the presentation on your laptop screen, and your audience will view the projected screen. Setting up dual-display mode and hooking up a projector to your Mac is straightforward; just follow these steps.

First, turn off the projector and computer.

Hook the projector up to the Mac. Apple laptops usually need an adapter to connect their VGA output to the projector's VGA input. Older iBooks, iBook G4, and 12" PowerBook G4 machines use the Apple mini-DVI to VGA adapter; the 15" and 17" PowerBook G4 machines use the Apple DVI to VGA adapter. All of these machines come with their respective adapters. The older Titanium Power-Book G4 laptops have a VGA port, so they don't need an adapter.

Turn on the projector and the computer. The Mac will recognize the existence of a second display and will go into mirrored mode, which puts the same image on the external display as is on the laptop's screen. Open System Preferences and choose Displays. In the Displays dialog, click the Display tab. Two windows will appear, one for each display. Click the window for the external display to bring it to the front.

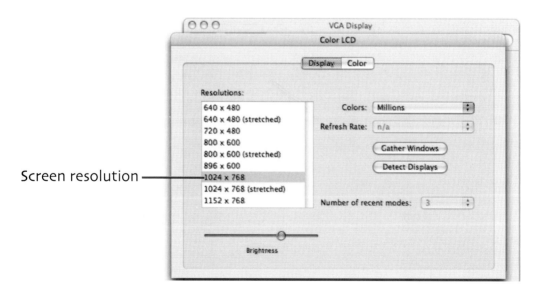

Screen resolution

deliver your presentation

Click the screen resolution that matches the resolution of the projector. If you don't know the projector's resolution, ask the person who supplied the projector, or just try different resolutions until you get a pleasing picture. It will typically be either 800 X 600 or 1024 X 768, so try those resolutions first. The two mirrored screens will change to the selected resolution.

If you don't want to use Keynote's Presenter Display, your setup is done. To use Presenter Display, you'll need to take the displays out of mirrored mode and into extended desktop mode, where the projector and laptop screen become one continuous desktop. If your Mac doesn't support extended desktop mode (iBooks, for example, only do mirroring), you can't use Presenter Display.

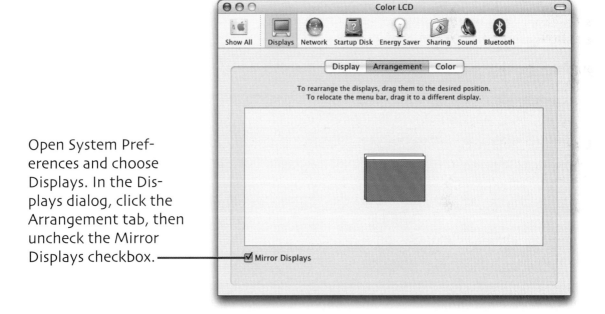

Open System Preferences and choose Displays. In the Displays dialog, click the Arrangement tab, then uncheck the Mirror Displays checkbox.

You can now set the resolution for each display separately. Click on the Display tab for each of the two display windows, and click the desired resolution.

set slideshow options

Now that you've set up your Mac for dual displays, you need to set up some preferences in Keynote. Choose Keynote > Preferences, then click the Slideshow button in the Preferences toolbar.

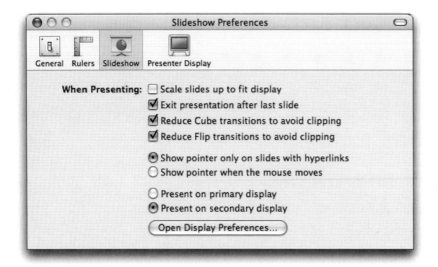

If your slides are smaller than the resolution of the projector, click Scale slides up to fit display to make them fill the screen. For example, some Keynote themes have 800 x 600 pixel slides. If you were to display the presentation on a 1024 x 768 projector, the presentation would appear with black borders around the edges. Choosing this option makes the presentation fit the resolution of the display screen.

The other option you'll want to set is Present on secondary display. This makes the presentation use the external projector or monitor when you are using a dual-display setup. Keynote considers the primary display to be the one with the menu bar.

If you'll be using the Presenter Display, you should customize what appears in it. In Keynote Preferences, click the Presenter Display button.

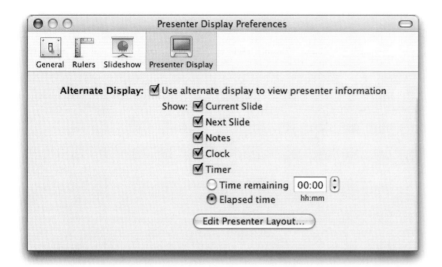

To turn on the Presenter Display, select Use alternate display to view presenter information. This will put the Presenter Display on your laptop screen while your presentation is running. You will see the Presenter Display, but your audience will not. You can choose to show the items listed in the dialog. To get an idea of what the Presenter Display will look like, click the Edit Presenter Layout button. You'll be taken to a preview of the Presenter Display that allows you to move and resize the items in the display to better match your working style. You'll learn more about the Presenter Display in the run the presentation section later in this chapter.

prepare yourself

So now you have created a terrific presentation, your laptop and the projector are set up, and your audience is beginning to drift into the room, eager for the show. But what about you? What about your needs? If you're like most people, you're feeling a little stage fright at this point. Dealing with your butterflies is what this section is about. Here are some tips that can help you keep your presentation running smoothly.

- Before the presentation, get a friend or coworker to read through your presentation. You'll be surprised at how often they'll find a typo or awkward grammar that you missed.

- If you can, get to the presentation venue early. Sit or stand where you will when you are speaking, and make sure that your seating (or the podium) is adjusted the way that you want it. Take a moment to adjust the microphone (if any) and work with the venue's audio technician to get the levels right before the audience arrives. Make sure you have a spot to place a cup of water. Getting comfortable with the physical space and facilities helps a lot.

- If you have the opportunity to greet some of the audience members as they enter the room, you should do so. It's easier to speak to people you know, even if all you've done is said hello.

- If you are speaking at a conference and you are wearing a conference badge or pass around your neck, take it off before you begin your talk. It will often reflect stage lights back at the audience, which can be distracting.

- Before you begin, visualize yourself giving a successful presentation. Imagine that you've spoken very well, and hear your audience's applause. Picture audience members coming up to congratulate you after the show. It sounds a bit silly, but visualizing success works.

- Concentrate on your message, not on the audience. If you focus on what you're saying, you will distract yourself from being nervous.

- If you are nervous, never apologize for it. Except in extreme cases, most audiences don't notice that speakers are nervous, and it doesn't help your case to point it out.

- Always keep in mind that your audience wants you to succeed. People don't go to a presentation thinking, "I sure hope this guy does a lousy talk and wastes my time." They want to get something out of your presentation as much as you do.

- Unless you are a professional comedian, keep the jokes to a minimum, or skip them altogether. A joke that falls flat isn't a good way to start a show.

- Never read straight from a script. Very few people can read from a script without putting their audience to sleep; we call those few people actors.

- Don't read your slides aloud word for word. Your slides should be signposts and reminders of what you want to say. Using your slides as a teleprompter is another way to lose audience interest. If you need prompting for your topics, use your speaker Notes.

- It's a good idea to put a summary slide at the end of your presentation. It brings your talk to a natural end, and it helps to once again drive your argument home to your audience.

- After the presentation is over, thank your audience and make yourself available for questions. Make sure to get feedback from them so that you can improve your next show.

run the presentation

To run the presentation, choose View > Play Slide-show, or click the Play button in the toolbar. Or you can press Control-Option-P on your keyboard.

The presentation appears on the screen. If you are using a projector or external monitor, the presentation appears on whichever screen you selected during set up.

During the presentation, Keynote provides some tools that you can use to control your show. They include ways to move to the previous and next slides, a field that allows you to jump to any slide in your presentation, and a way to pause your presentation or turn the screen black for a moment.

To bring up the slide switcher during a presentation, type a slide number, or press the plus sign, equals sign, or hyphen on your keyboard. The slide switcher appears as an overlay on your slide. If you are using the Presenter Display, the slide switcher will overlay that display instead.

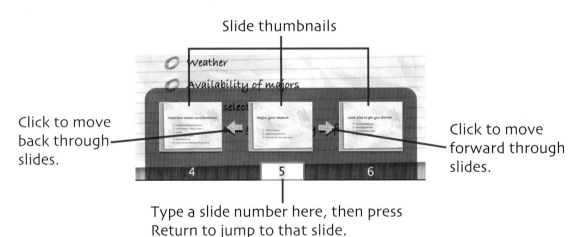

Slide thumbnails

Click to move back through slides.

Click to move forward through slides.

Type a slide number here, then press Return to jump to that slide.

Click a slide thumbnail to close the slide switcher and go to that slide. To close the slide switcher without changing the current slide, press the Esc key.

To advance to the next slide or slide build, click the mouse button, press Return, press N, or press the Right Arrow key on the keyboard. To return to a previous slide, press Delete, press P, or press the Left Arrow key.

At the end of the show, by default you drop out of Slideshow mode and go back to the Keynote window automatically when you advance past the last slide. You can prevent that by clearing the Exit presentation after last slide checkbox in the Slideshow pane of Keynote's Preferences. If you do that, you can't advance past the last slide; you must leave the presentation by pressing Esc.

When Presenting: ☐ Scale slides up to fit display
☐ Exit presentation after last slide

To end the slideshow manually at any time, press Esc, Q, Command-period, or just the period key.

During the presentation, you can also get some additional features from the keyboard.

shortcut	what it does
home	go to first slide
end	go to last slide
F	pause presentation
B	pause presentation and turn screen black
?	bring up keyboard shortcuts help screen
R	reset timer (in Presenter Display)
U	scroll speaker Notes up (in Presenter Display)
D	scroll speaker Notes down (in Presenter Display)

use presenter display

Presenter Display is a new feature that gives you more control over the presentation as you are giving it. It gives you a control panel that you see on your laptop's screen, while the audience sees the regular slideshow on the projector. This mode is only available when you are using multiple monitors in extended desktop mode. This means that iBooks, iMacs, and eMacs cannot use the Presenter Display, because they can only use mirrored mode.

In Presenter View, you get large views of the current and next slides or slide builds, your speaker Notes, a clock, and best of all, an on-screen timer that tells you either the elapsed time of your presentation or a countdown of the time remaining. This timer is a great tool to help you stay on track; by knowing how long you have been talking, you can speed up or slow down to keep within your allotted speaking time.

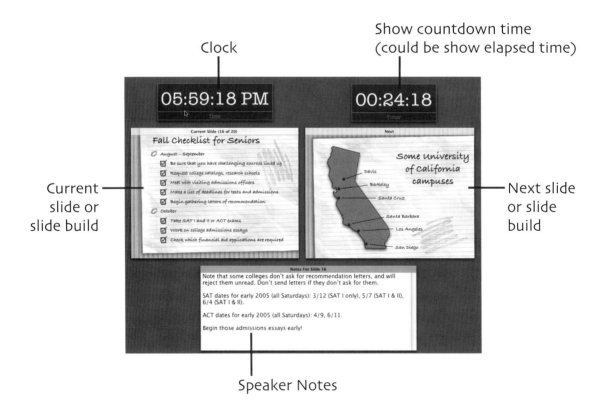

Clock

Show countdown time
(could be show elapsed time)

Current slide or slide build

Next slide or slide build

Speaker Notes

When using the Presenter Display, the Current Slide window always shows you what the audience is seeing on the projector, and the Next window shows what will happen next. If you have slide builds in your presentation, you'll need to get used to the fact that the Next window shows you the result of the next build, not always the next slide. For example, slide 14 shows in the Current Slide window what is showing on the main presentation screen, before the slide build that animates the chart onto the slide, which shows in the Next window.

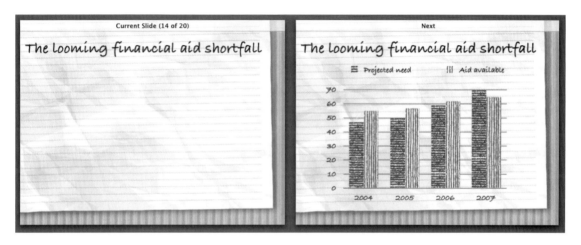

Audience is seeing this screen

What the audience will see after you press the Right Arrow key to trigger the chart build

extra bits

set up the projector p. 108

- Most of the time, you don't actually have to turn the computer and projector off before you hook them together. You can connect them, then open the Displays pane of System Preferences. If two display windows don't appear, click the Detect Displays button, which will scan for displays, after which the second display window will appear. If that doesn't work, then try turning things off and on again.

prepare yourself p. 112

- If you want to become a better presenter, there are some terrific online resources. I'm a fan of the Beyond Bullets weblog (www. beyondbullets.com), written by Cliff Atkinson. It's full of practical tips and information that will help you think about doing presentations in a different way. It's aimed at PowerPoint users, but most of the stories and tips on the site aren't specific to any one brand of presentation software.

- The best presentation I've ever seen didn't use a single bullet point. It was performed by Scott McCloud, who wrote Understanding Comics (1993, Perennial Currents), a brilliant, essential

book that will help you understand all forms of visual communications, including presentation software like Keynote and PowerPoint. And it's mostly done as comics! Trust me on this one.

run the presentation p. 114

- If you are presenting on an iBook, an iMac, or an eMac, which are only capable of mirrored video mode, you will not be able to see your speaker Notes on the laptop screen.

- Keynote 2's new Presenter Display is useful while you're giving a talk, but there's no preview in Presenter mode, as there is in PowerPoint's similar feature, so you usually need an external monitor or projector to practice your presentation. But you can trick Keynote into letting you practice in front of the Presenter Display without a projector.

  Plug the video dongle you use to hook up a projector into your laptop, then open Displays in System Preferences and uncheck "Mirror Displays" on the Arrangement tab. Launch Keynote, and choose Keynote > Preferences.

  On the Slideshow pane, click Present on secondary display, and on the Presenter Display

deliver your presentation

tab, click Use alternate display to view presenter information. Then close the Preferences window. When you play your presentation, you'll see the Presenter Display on your laptop screen.

- Besides clicking the mouse or pressing the Right Arrow key, you can also use the spacebar to advance slides or perform the next slide build. I usually use the spacebar when I present, because it's the biggest and easiest to find by touch while I'm talking.

- There are a few great hardware accessories that can help almost any presentation. The first is an inexpensive laser pointer. These are essential for drawing your audience's attention to a part of your slide. I have a fancy (and pricy) laser pointer with a green beam, but that's because I'm a presentation geek. You can find the standard models with red beams for as little as $10. You can also benefit from a remote control for your computer, because they allow you to wirelessly roam anywhere on the stage, rather than being tied to your laptop. These units usually consist of a handheld control and a receiver that connects to your laptop via the USB port. Some of

them, such as units from Keyspan (www.keyspan.com) and Targus (www.targus.com), have a built-in laser pointer. Just make sure that the remote is Mac-compatible (most are).

- You may already have a perfectly good remote control for your Mac without even knowing it. It's your mobile phone. Yes, that's right. If your phone and laptop both have Bluetooth, you can control Keynote with it, as long as you pick up a software package called Salling Clicker, from Salling Software (www.salling.com). Clicker breaks the shackles that tie you to your laptop; you can roam up to 30 feet away and still control the laptop. Clicker controls a wide range of programs on the Mac, including Keynote, PowerPoint, iTunes, and almost any other program that uses AppleScript.

extra bits

use presenter display p. 116

- I find that the countdown timer is more useful than the elapsed time counter. For me, it's better to know how much time I have left, rather than how long I've been talking.

- Unfortunately, you can't type new notes or change your speaker Notes during the show.

deliver your presentation

10. present everywhere

Given the smashing success of your presentation, chances are good that you'll be asked to provide it to others or take it on the road. As usual, Keynote is up to the task. You can convert the presentation into a QuickTime or Macromedia Flash movie, or you can even save the show as Web pages that can be viewed by anyone with a Web browser.

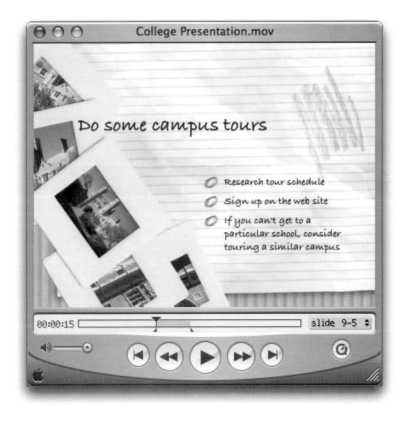

save as quicktime movie

You can save the presentation as a QuickTime movie, which can be played on any computer that has the QuickTime Player installed (all Macs have this, and QuickTime is often installed on Windows machines). The main benefit is that your presentation can be played on Macs that don't have Keynote installed, or any Windows machine with QuickTime. Keynote files exported as QuickTime movies include all the transitions and animated object builds that you added to the presentation.

You can create an interactive QuickTime movie, which allows your viewers to advance through the slide builds and slides manually, much as you would when you give the presentation. Alternatively, you can create a self-playing QuickTime movie, which is useful for unattended presentations, such as kiosks. When you create a self-running QuickTime movie, you can set the duration for object builds and how long a slide is visible.

With either kind of QuickTime movie, you can decide the size of the movie file, from full-sized movies (with the video the same size as your slides), down to small movies optimized for use on Web sites.

1 To convert a presentation to a QuickTime movie, choose File > Export. The Export dialog will appear. Click the QuickTime radio button, then click Next.

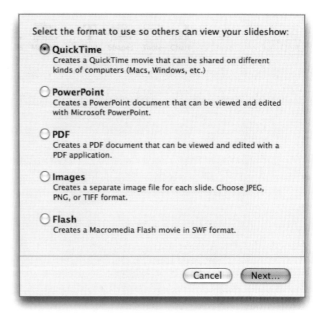

The QuickTime settings dialog appears.

2 Choose Interactive Slideshow or Self-Playing Movie from this pop-up menu.

3 For interactive movies, these options are unavailable. For self-playing movies, set the slide and build durations. From the Repeat pop-up menu, you can also choose None, Loop (makes the presentation play continuously), or Back and Forth (makes the presentation play through once, then, when it reaches the end, begin to play backwards).

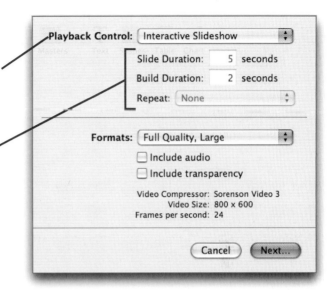

4 From the Formats pop-up menu, choose one of the following presets:

Full Quality, Large uses the Sorenson Video 3 video compressor, at 24 frames per second (fps), and produces movies that are the same size as your slides. Use this one for the highest quality presentations. The tradeoff is that this option creates the largest files.

CD-ROM Movie, Medium uses the same video compressor at half the frame rate, and the movie is half the size. So if your slides are 800 x 600 pixels, the movie will be 400 x 300.

Web Movie, Small uses the same video compressor and frame rate as the Medium setting, but the movie is one-quarter the Large size.

5 If you have audio in your presentation that you want included in the movie, check Include audio. The Include transparency option preserves transparent objects on your slides.

continues on next page

present everywhere

save as quicktime movie

6 Click Next. A Save As dialog will appear. Name the movie, navigate to where you want the movie to be saved, and click the Export button. Keynote will export the movie, showing you a progress dialog as the export proceeds.

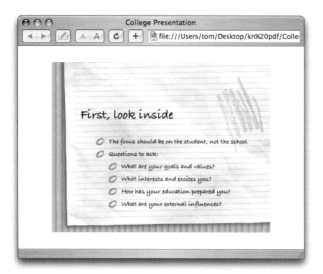

To play back the movie, double-click it to launch QuickTime Player, or drag it into a new (empty) Safari window to see it in a browser. If it is an interactive movie, you can click in the movie window to advance the slideshow. A self-playing movie will, of course, begin playing.

save as flash movie

New to Keynote 2 is the ability to export files in Macromedia Flash format. This allows the presentation to be viewed in any Web browser that supports Flash (virtually all browsers), as well as the Macromedia Flash Player 7. The presentation will appear in the Flash Player at full size, and will act as an interactive slideshow. Because the Flash format is a bit more efficient than QuickTime, the file size will be smaller. The drawback is that the presentation will not have the same fidelity as the QuickTime version. Slide builds will usually work fine, but Flash can't replicate all of Keynote's transitions correctly, embedded QuickTime movies won't play, and custom bullets will not appear the way they do in Keynote or QuickTime. Flash playback may be better in some situations, however, so it is an option you should consider.

Slide in Flash Player 7; note the generic bullets

The same slide in Keynote, with the correct custom bullets

continues on next page

save as flash movie (cont.)

1 To convert a presentation to a Flash movie, choose File > Export. The Export dialog will appear. Click the Flash radio button, then click Next.

2 A Save As dialog will appear. Name the Flash movie, navigate to where you want the movie to be saved, and click the Export button. Keynote will export the movie, showing you a progress dialog as the export proceeds.

present everywhere

save as web site

You can make your presentation available to the widest audience by converting it into a Web site and placing it on a Web server, either on the Internet or on your company's intranet. The presentation will be readable by anyone with a Web browser on any major computing platform (Windows, Mac, Linux, and others).

Unfortunately, Keynote can't handle Web export by itself, so you'll need to use a handy shareware program, KeyWebX, by Michael Samarin (www.keywebx.com). This program can't read Keynote presentation files directly; you will first need to export the file as a PDF or as an interactive QuickTime movie. I've found that PDF works more reliably, so that's the method we'll use here. With PDF export, each slide is exported as a different page in the PDF file, after all slide builds for that slide are completed.

1 To convert a presentation to a PDF, choose File > Export. The Export dialog will appear. Click the PDF radio button, then click Next.

2 A Save As dialog will appear. Name the PDF file, navigate to where you want it to be saved, and click the Export button. Keynote will export the file, showing you a progress dialog as the export proceeds.

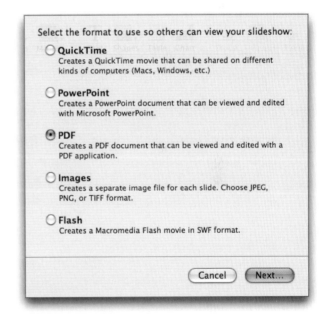

Select the format to use so others can view your slideshow:

○ **QuickTime**
Creates a QuickTime movie that can be shared on different kinds of computers (Macs, Windows, etc.)

○ **PowerPoint**
Creates a PowerPoint document that can be viewed and edited with Microsoft PowerPoint.

⦿ **PDF**
Creates a PDF document that can be viewed and edited with a PDF application.

○ **Images**
Creates a separate image file for each slide. Choose JPEG, PNG, or TIFF format.

○ **Flash**
Creates a Macromedia Flash movie in SWF format.

(Cancel) (Next...)

continues on next page

save as web site (cont.)

3 Launch KeyWebX. The processing window appears.

4 In the Step 1 area, choose PDF file (Keynote or AppleWorks export) from the pop-up menu.

5 Click the Select button, and from the resulting Open dialog, select the PDF file you want to convert to a Web site.

6 In the Step 2 section, enter the Image Width and Image Height (I find that the default values are good), then choose an HTML Template from the pop-up menu. This will determine the look of the Web site.

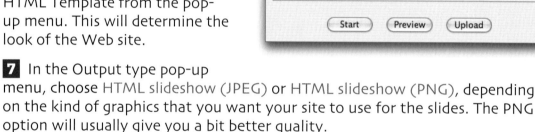

7 In the Output type pop-up menu, choose HTML slideshow (JPEG) or HTML slideshow (PNG), depending on the kind of graphics that you want your site to use for the slides. The PNG option will usually give you a bit better quality.

8 In the Step 4 area, click the Select button to specify in an Open dialog where you want the converted images and files to be placed.

9 Click the Start button. A dialog will appear asking you to give the slideshow a title. Do so, then click OK. The PDF file will be processed into a Web site.

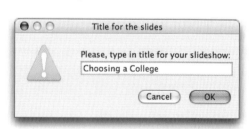

The resulting Web site will appear in the output folder you picked.

Once the site has been created, you can preview it by clicking the Preview button in KeyWebX, or double-click the index.html file in the output folder to see the site in your default Web browser.

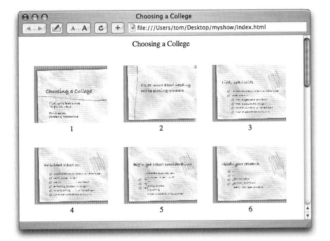

The index page of the site shows thumbnails of all the slides in your slideshow.

Clicking a thumbnail brings you to a detail page with Previous and Next buttons.

You need to copy the Web page and the companion folder to a Web server for it to be viewable by others. If you don't know how to do that, ask your Web site's administrator.

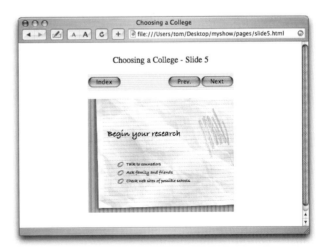

extra bits

save as quicktime movie p. 122

- Keep in mind that if you include audio in your presentation it can significantly increase the file size, especially if you have a soundtrack throughout your slideshow.

- By default, interactive movies will not show the familiar QuickTime movie controller in either a browser or the QuickTime Player. You can change that by downloading a package of QuickTime AppleScripts from www.apple.com/applescript/quicktime/. Among the many AppleScripts in this collection is one called Set Controller Type. Double-click the script, and you'll see a Set Prefs button. Click this button, and in the resulting dialog set the controller type to Standard. Then, in the Finder, drag the exported movie onto the Set Controller Type script icon. The script will run and enable the controller, as shown here. Self-playing movies will always show the controller.

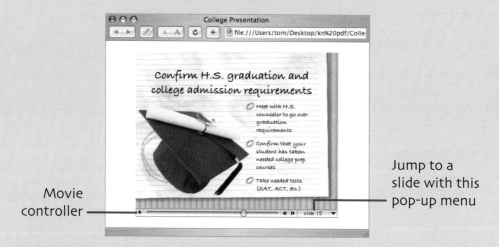

Movie controller

Jump to a slide with this pop-up menu

- I found a small bug in the Set Controller Type script mentioned above, so I have fixed it and uploaded the fixed script to this book's companion Web site, at www.negrino.com/keynote-vqj/. Feel free to download the script from that page instead.

- One easy way to transport your exported presentations is to burn the Quick-Time movie to a CD, or copy it onto one of the popular USB flash memory keychain drives, or even use your iPod or iPod shuffle.

- If you will be showing your converted slideshow on a Windows machine, you may need to install QuickTime for Windows. You can download the free Windows QuickTime player from http://www.apple.com/quicktime/download/.

- If you want to play back your exported presentation movies in full screen mode (where the movie takes over the entire screen), you will need to purchase the QuickTime Pro upgrade from the Apple Store online. This costs $30, but it's well worth the cost. Besides being able to play back in full screen (which is almost as good as having Keynote installed), QuickTime Pro also lets you save movies from the Web; do simple editing of any kind of video or audio content that QuickTime supports; and convert media from one sort of format to others.

save as flash movie p. 125

- Make sure that you don't try to play back the Flash movie in the QuickTime Player or a Flash Player version before 7; you will not get a good result. These players will replace every space in your slide text with &20, making slides unreadable. You can only play back exported presentations in Flash format with the Flash Player 7 or later.

- Keynote presentations that contain only vector drawings (not, for example, photographs) will export better to Flash, and the Flash movie will be scalable without loss of quality.

- If Flash movies don't play with the same fidelity as QuickTime, you might be wondering why you would ever want to use them. Here are two reasons: first, you might be in a situation where you are required to produce Flash output, for use on the Web, for example, or so your presentation can be included in a larger Flash project. Second, Keynote is much less expensive than Macromedia Flash MX, so you can produce Flash output on the cheap.

extra bits

save as web site p. 127

- The KeyWebX User Manual explains how to make your own HTML templates if you wish to customize the look of your Web site.

- You can easily add text notes (which are not the same as your Keynote speaker Notes), audio annotations, or video clips to the Web pages you create with KeyWebX. See the KeyWebX User Manual for the details.

- If you are a .Mac member, it is easy to publish your KeyWebX-generated Web site. Simply mount your iDisk by switching to the Finder and choosing Go > iDisk > My iDisk, then drag the KeyWebX output folder and its contents into the Sites folder on your iDisk. If the name of the output folder were presentation, the URL of your slideshow will then be http://homepage.mac.com/yourusername/presentation/, where yourusername would be, of course, your .Mac user name.

appendix: theme showcase

One of the great things about using Keynote is that there are many excellent themes available for you to use in your presentations. Shortly after Keynote was released, a lively community of theme makers sprang up to push the envelope for themes past the twenty theme examples that Apple supplies with the program.

For additional help with Keynote, check out these two resources:

Apple's Keynote discussion forums, at http://discussions.info.apple.com/keynote/ have lots of volunteer Keynote experts hanging around to help you out.

If you prefer to get your assistance from a mailing list, take a look at the Keynote Yahoo! Group, at http://groups.yahoo.com/group/applekeynote/.

I've listed these Keynote theme developers in alphabetical order. I urge you to visit each of these sites to see all of the themes that are available.

keynote developers

Jumsoft www.jumsoft.com

Both of these examples are from Jumsoft's Keynote Themes 4.0 collection, which contains 27 different themes at an attractive price.

The Color theme contains 13 different master slides, and comes in 1024 x 768 and 800 x 600 sizes.

The GridWay theme contains 11 master slides, and sports a clean, businesslike look.

Keynote Gallery www.keynotegallery.com

Keynote Gallery offers a wide selection of themes, with many different looks. Some of their themes are available in collections, often at substantial savings.

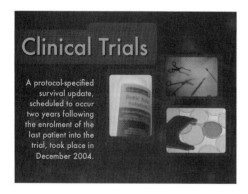

The Molecular theme contains 27 different master slides, with custom chart fills and custom bullets.

Portfolio includes 34 master slides and lots of extras, and has many master slides with different custom photo cutouts. It's great for photo-heavy presentations.

theme showcase

Keynote HQ www.keynotehq.com

Keynote HQ offers several theme packs, including some themes designed for specialized uses such as church presentations. All of the themes are available in both 1024 x 768 and 800 x 600 sizes.

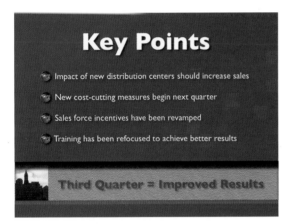

The Blue Abstract theme includes 35 different master slides, many with photo cutouts that have nicely beveled edges, as shown here. Extras in the theme include custom bullets, background textures, and other objects.

Masterpiece features master slides with a base texture that looks like an artist's canvas. You can add in special touches like paint-glob bullets, "painted" title bars, and matching canvas chart fills to create a unique look in your presentations.

keynote developers (cont.)

Keynote Pro www.keynotepro.com

Keynote Pro lives up to its name, with a terrific selection of themes that will make your ideas look sleek and professional. This site, along with KeynoteUser and Keynote Theme Park, is really pushing the edges of what you can do with Keynote.

The Keystation theme is the first to be released that was designed to take advantage of Keynote 2's new ability for interactive and unattended kiosk presentations. Available in regular and HD sizes (for widescreen monitors), you can rapidly customize the presentation with a simple background color change or via Keynote-native shape objects and fills. The kiosk-mode master slides include interface-oriented elements such as menu screens, directories, and galleries.

The Pavilion theme is inspired by the classic sophistication of Deco-styled glass-on-post panels in a modernist interpretation with modern type and layout, set against a background of polished aluminum.

theme showcase

Keynote Theme Park www.keynotethemepark.com

Wow You Designs produces a great selection of beautifully designed themes, with plenty of attention to detail. The themes all include custom bullets and chart fills designed especially to match the theme.

The unique Reflections theme gives the appearance of content reflecting on a highly polished surface. Reflections includes 22 photo cutout master slides (plus 8 text) that come in both black and white for a total of 60 masters. Designed specifically for Keynote 2, it has a selection of interactive buttons for use with Keynote's new hyperlink tool.

The TecTile theme works in tandem with Keynote's Mosaic transition. It's based on a grid of squares that are sized and positioned to match the flipping tiles of the transition. Each tile can be deleted or have its opacity adjusted by the user to allow images to show through. This innovative theme also comes with lots of extras.

keynote developers (cont.)

KeynoteUser www.keynoteuser.com

KeynoteUser was one of the first theme sites, and its themes are exhaustive in scope and attention to detail. It is also a Keynote news site and operates the popular Keynote Yahoo! Mailing list.

The Candy 2 theme requires Keynote 2 (an older version supports the older Keynote) and provides a colorful look inspired by Mac OS X itself. It also includes a cool supplemental set of master slides called Candy Machine, which allows you to make your own custom photo cutout slides.

The Frames theme isn't just another theme. It's a whole system that contains almost 100 different slide layouts in four styles. Also included are lots of extra slide building parts, more bullets than you can imagine, a sample file filled with free images and cool ideas, and tutorials on how to create your own photo cutouts using a drawing program like Macromedia FreeHand or Adobe Illustrator. Many of the frames and cutouts bleed off the edge of the slide, so you can use Keynote transitions to make it look as though different sides are connected.

index

index

index

index

index

W

Web sites
    downloading free clip art, 25
    exporting presentations as,
        127–129, 132
    finding more themes, 38
    finding royalty-free sound
        on, 26, 27
    opening from slide hyperlink,
        51–52, 56
    PowerPoint Art, 38
    publishing KeyWebX-
        generated, 132
    reviewing PDF presentations
        from, 104
    searching for royalty-free
        images, 27
    searching for slide
        backgrounds, 38
Web views
    adding drop shadows for, 76
    inserting in presentation, 69
    updating, 76
windows
    Keynote, 2
    opening multiple inspector,
        11
Windows QuickTime players,
    131
writing presentations, 13–19
    changing font size, 19, 43
    creating additional slides, 15
    moving headings and
        subheadings, 16
    OmniOutliner, 18
    Outline view for, 14–15
    printing outlines, 19, 105
    titles, headings, and
        subheadings, 14–15

Z

.zip files, 94, 104
Zoom menu, 8, 27